GREAT YACHTS

315

GREAT YACHTS

Lord Feversham

with contributions from
Ronald Faux, John Liley,
Christopher Penfold and
Douglas Phillips-Birt

Advisory Editor
William W. Robinson

G. P. Putnam's Sons
New York

Library of Congress Catalog Card Number: 76–127715

Printed in Great Britain

Contents

Introduction

YACHTING IS ONE OF THE WORLD'S GROWTH SPORTS. HIGHER LIVING STANDARDS SINCE THE Second World War linked with an increase in time for leisure has had an explosive effect on the participant sports. The expansion in the pleasure boat industry at popular level has seen the mushrooming of dinghy fleets world wide, while the stress in the development of cruising yacht design is for small, relatively cheap but safe family boats both under sail and power. The use of new materials and production line methods in boat building have brought yachting within the reach of a wide public.

A number of factors contributed to the steady growth of yachting during the nineteenth century, after rather uncertain beginnings. Behind the whole movement lurked the irresistible fascination of the sea, presenting a challenge for man to master the elements and to satisfy man's inherent inquisitiveness through exploration. These basic motives for yachting were fired by the spirit of competition. Although yachting became a rich man's sport emancipation to its current popularity was the direct result of intense competition between the two great yachting nations, The United States of America and Great Britain. The design techniques evolved for the vast America's Cup yachts of the ninteen twenties and thirties, when the terms of competition were hardly restricted financially and the 'sky was the limit', are relevant to the mass production yachts of the modern yachting world. The current status of the sport is the result of 150 years of continuous advance in design thinking. The competitive sector in yachting remains the development area in terms of design. It is in the field of ocean racing and offshore powerboat racing that yachting progress continues to be made.

Great yachts stand out in history as pace setters in a design race, where the aim is for speed and efficiency combined with safety. However, the character of a yacht is more complex than that and cannot be judged only on the merits of its design or on its competition record. Yachts are remembered for a variety of reasons ranging from the absurd, the eccentricity of an owner, perhaps, to the purely practical. This book traces the history of yachting through some of those yachts which have left their mark on the sport. For one reason or another they are the Great Yachts.

In selecting the yachts to be included in this book great care has been taken to relate them specifically to the development of the sport as a whole. They have been chosen not only to pinpoint the innovation of great design techniques but also to illustrate the various characteristics and attitudes of designers and yachtsmen at different periods of yachting history, to give the feel of the steam yacht era or a lone voyage round the world. The aim has been to cover the whole field of yachting activity throughout the world from the humble 14 ft. sailing dinghy to the royal steam yachts, exceeding 2,000 tons. The wide-ranging nature of this approach has necessitated extreme care in sifting out technical information which is relevant to the general development of yachting from a wealth of detail, of significance for instance in a particular sphere such as the America's Cup competition, but less important in a broad view of the sport.

In analysis every yachtsman's greatest yacht is the one he owns himself, whether he is challenging for the America's Cup or weekending with his family aboard his glass-fibre cabin cruiser. The great yachts in this book show just how his great yacht came to be the shape it is and how it performs the way it does.

I would like to thank all those who have helped me collate and sift the vast amount of information, the numerous yacht designers, yachtsmen and yachting historians on both sides of the Atlantic who have given their time and the benefit of their knowledge to the project. In particular I should like to thank Bill Robinson, who has acted as American Advisory Editor, and the various named experts who have contributed to the text for their co-operation. I am grateful to John Nicholson for his advice to me in compiling the chapters on steam and motor yachts and to Renato Levi for furnishing me with details of his design for *Cohete*. I should like to acknowledge also the work of John G. D. Henderson, who checked my information with his impressive collection of Lloyds Registers, and Mr J. D. Calder, O.B.E. whose advice, based on 70 years in the boating industry, was of great value to me. Finally I should like to thank the Editor for allowing me access to the bound volumes of *Motor Boat and Yachting* where, amongst other items of importance, I discovered the original boat test report of 1913 for *Pioneer*, the world's first diesel yacht.

Early Yachts

IT IS NOT EASY TO PINPOINT A DATE WHEN BOATING EMERGED AS A LEISURETIME ACTIVITY. Early civilizations constructed boats which were capable of extensive deep-sea voyaging. However, little evidence exists to show that these voyages were made for fun and difficulty arises during the early years of nautical history in discriminating between the multitude of small workboats, employed in fishing or carrying cargo, and those isolated vessels used purely for pleasure.

Biblical references show that boats were regarded as a particularly dangerous form of travel, or a precarious means of earning a livelihood, and clearly St Paul was not engaged on a pleasure cruise when he was shipwrecked. Nevertheless, it does seem likely that for as long as man has been building workboats and launching them on to the stormy sea, there have been moments of calm when the holds have been empty of cargo, the fishing nets have been drawn in, and boating has become a pleasure. There is no doubt, for instance, that yachts existed in ancient Egypt. The earliest evidence of a yacht is provided by a model, discovered in an Egyptian tomb, which shows that there was at least one 100-ft. vessel, with a cabin and used for pleasure purposes, on the Nile in 1500 B.C. Although discoveries of this kind show that yachts existed centuries before Christ, it is not until much later that we find evidence of any yachting activity on a notable scale, and many historians judge yachting in its modern form to have been founded on the lakes and rivers of seventeenth-century Holland.

The geography of Holland, woven in a labyrinth of waterways, made travel difficult without boats. Many Dutchmen living in the seventeenth century needed a boat for a simple journey which in England or France would have been undertaken on horseback. The fact that the Dutch used a boat rather than a horse to carry their cabbages to market and their families to dinner with neighbours, led not only to boating for pleasure but to the construction of boats primarily for that purpose. A special craft of this nature was called a 'jaght' and, of course, it is from this early Dutch word that our 'yacht' is derived.

If yachting became something of a social phenomenon in seventeenth-century Holland, it is important to remember that the distinction between workboats and pleasure boats continued to be a fine one for the best part of another two centuries. Doubtless the early Dutch jaghts doubled as workboats and personal conveyances for their owners, while in wartime they would have been seconded into service with the Dutch Navy. Wherever foreigners who visited Holland carried the notion of yachting back to their own countries, where the boat was not an accepted form of everyday transport, the use of the boat for pleasure continued to be regarded as remarkable.

Perhaps the most notable individual to extend yachting outside Holland was Charles II, king of England. Charles had spent some time living in exile in the Low Countries before being restored to the English throne in May 1660. Three months after the Restoration when, after dinner on 15th August, Samuel Pepys called at Whitehall, he found 'the king gone this morning by 5 of the clock to see a Dutch pleasure boat below the bridge'. This boat was the *Mary,* a present to Charles from the city of Amsterdam and a typical Dutch state yacht.

(on previous two pages) **Gretel**, the first Australian challenger for the America's Cup.

(left) A regatta of the **Cumberland Fleet** at Blackfriars under the shadow of St. Paul's. The founding of the fleet by the Duke of Cumberland in 1775 was the beginning of sustained interest in yachting in England.

She was 66 ft. long with a beam of $18\frac{1}{2}$ ft., and had been built originally for the Dutch East India Company.

The shrewd Dutch merchants who gave *Mary* to Charles, had been quick to notice the taste for sailing which he had shown during his exile in their country. Certainly, *Mary* was a pretty enough little vessel to appeal to a king. The figurehead was a unicorn and the royal arms of England were emblazoned on the stern. The high coach roof and side windows of the stern cabin were covered in ornate carving. Eight ornamental cannon projected from the gun ports, decorated with gilded wreaths.

Dutch merchants also gave a smaller yacht, the *Bezan*, to Charles and he himself bought, for sentimental reasons, the little smack *Surprise*, in which he had escaped to France from Brighton after his defeat at the battle of Worcester.

These first Dutch yachts, broad of beam and with little draught, were fitted with lee-boards to enable them to sail to windward in the shallow waters of their native Holland. Encouraged by royal patronage, English shipwrights soon began to design and build craft which were more suitable for deeper English waters. Between 1661 and 1663 Peter and Christopher Pett and Master Thomas Shish designed five new royal yachts which were all based on the lines of contemporary English warships.

Evelyn records in his diary a race sailed between the King's *Katherine* and the Duke of York's *Anne*, for a wager of £100, from Greenwich to Gravesend and back. The king, he wrote, lost it going, the wind being contrary, but saved the stakes in returning. There were divers noble persons and lords on board, His Majesty sometimes steering himself. His barge

Lord Yarborough's 351 ton **Falcon** was typical of the larger early 19th century yachts. Fully rigged, she resembled a man o' war in miniature.

and kitchen boat attended. (These kitchen boats were specially designed to accommodate the royal cooks, and were vessels of about 101 tons, 51 ft. in length with a beam of 19 ft. 4 in.)

Another favourite Stuart yacht was the *Fubbs,* which was the King's pet name for the Duchess of Portsmouth. *Fubbs* was built by Sir Phineas Pett and was the first yacht to be rigged as a ketch, without a foremast. Charles took a personal interest in her building, even claiming that he was the inventor of the two-masted rig. Certainly the King's passion for yachting and his interest in naval architecture was largely responsible for the progress made in ship design during his reign. At one time he had no fewer than fifteen royal yachts in commission, all paid for out of the privy purse, ranging in size from the *Portsmouth* of 133 tons to the little 24-tonner, *Deal.*

Samuel Pepys often complained at his master's extravagance when he was secretary at the Admiralty, although it is hard to see that his grounds for so doing were justified. The King's delight in yachting supported his desire to maintain his country as a great sea power. It is the custom of the English, he told Louis XIV's ambassador to Whitehall, to command at sea. When he tired of a royal yacht it was turned over immediately for service with the Navy.

After the death of Charles II in 1685, royal patronage of yachting in England lost much of its early fervour and activity declined. No new boats were commissioned during the short reign of James II and it took a Dutchman, in the shape of William III, who with his wife Mary succeeded James to the English throne, to reintroduce yachting to England. Even William was not the enthusiast that Charles II had been. He did not commission a host of new yachts as Charles had done. He did not race up and down the Thames for wagers, accompanied by kitchen boats. Nevertheless he did bring with him from Holland a remarkable vessel for use as a royal yacht, called *Princess Mary.*

The *Princess Mary* was used as a royal yacht by William, Queen Anne and George I, ending her long life as a collier and provoking the couplet,

> Behold the fate of sublunary things;
> She exports coal which once imported Kings.

At the end *Princess Mary,* by now lurking under the humble guise of *Betsy Cairns,* hit a reef in foul weather off the mouth of the Tyne. She sank in 1827, having survived 139 years of Kings and coals.

The death of Charles II put an end to any extensive development of yachting as a pastime in England and ninety years were to elapse before the start of an era which saw Britain as a world pioneer of the sport. However, it would be wrong to ignore the early Dutch influence in the use of boats for pleasure, for British yachting did not die out altogether. As royal yacht for three reigns, *Princess Mary* provided a thread of continuity during the intervening period. But when the historian Macaulay describes Caermarthen, a son of the Duke of Leeds, as being somewhat eccentric because he owned a small yacht of marvellous speed, it shows that William and Mary, Queen Anne and George I were lukewarm yachtsmen and that their influence in this field did not extend very far. To Macaulay and the vast majority of his Victorian contemporaries the yachtsman had become an odd fish by the first half of the eighteenth century.

The next outburst of organized yachting enthusiasm took place in Ireland. Ireland holds an important place in yachting history for it was in this country that the yacht club first appeared. In 1720 the Water Club of the Harbour of Cork was founded. It consisted of twenty-five members whose pleasure it was to go cruising with their yachts in company, dress up in fancy uniforms, hoist a great many signals, fire cannons, eat, drink and make merry. If Macaulay found Caermarthen somewhat eccentric he would have described members of the Cork Water Club as lunatics for having such fun, but their activities passed from strength to strength. The uniforms became fancier, the cannons fired louder, the eating and drinking went better, the merriment grew and the Club flourished until 1765. Efforts were made to revive it at the beginning of the nineteenth century, when another club was formed, The Little Monkstown, by a few survivors of the old Water Club. Later the right to use the title of Royal Cork Yacht Club was granted to its members and as such it exists today, the oldest yacht club in the world. Another early Irish yacht club was founded in 1770 on Lough Ree, one of the two huge freshwater lakes in the Shannon River complex.

Surprisingly, the clubable English remained impervious to all this activity in the far flung Irish corner of the kingdom and it took a new royal enthusiast to jolt them out of their lethargy. Under the royal patronage of Henry Frederick, Duke of Cumberland, the Cumberland fleet was founded in 1775. Its purpose was to promote regattas or 'water parties' as they were known, for the large number of small craft afloat on the River Thames. Interest in yachting on the Thames had started to build up once again when in 1749 a race was sailed from Greenwich to the Nore and back for a plate presented by the Prince of Wales, but it was not until the Cumberland Fleet came into existence that any firm shape was given to the sport. In fact the Duke of Cumberland and his friends laid the foundation of the sport of yacht racing as it is known today. Their water parties were held between Blackfriars and Putney, and when they were tired of sailing they adjourned to Mr Smith's Tea Gardens at Vauxhall, the proprietor of which became the first Commodore of the Cumberland Fleet. It is significant that in spite of royal patronage the membership of the fleet was not made up predominantly of the aristocracy or of courtiers. Far more it provided relaxation for Londoners, business and professional men, who moored their small craft at the Temple Stairs, and the city merchants with their country houses overlooking Chelsea Reach.

In 1823, the Fleet's name was changed to His Majesty's Coronation Society, in honour of the crowning of George IV, but the society was short-lived, because of a protest case between yachts competing in the very first race sailed under the new title. Those members who disagreed with the committee's findings in the dispute held a meeting at the White Horse Tavern and formed the Thames Yacht Club, now the Royal Thames Yacht Club. Many of the cups raced for by the Cumberland Fleet can still be seen, together with a set of the Fleet flags, at the premises of the Royal Thames Yacht Club in Knightsbridge, London. But if the Duke of Cumberland and his relatively humble friends in London had given the initial shove to start the ball rolling, it was not long before the wealthy and more ambitious members of the aristocracy were throwing their impetus behind the movement.

On 1st June 1815 a number of nobles and gentlemen, under the chairmanship of Lord Grantham, had assembled at the Thatched House Tavern, in St James's Street, London, to found a new yacht club. Two years later, a special meeting of its members was called at East Cowes so that Sir Arthur Paget could read a letter, written by the Regent from his yacht, the *Royal George,* stating his desire to join the club. In 1818 the Royal Princes, the Dukes of Clarence and Gloucester also became members, and when the Regent became King in 1820, he gave his consent for the club to call itself the Royal Yacht Club, the first yacht club to enjoy this distinction. The next fifty years saw the formation of yacht clubs throughout the world. England, with her far flung colonies, was in a position to lead the way and Royal Yacht Clubs were founded in Gibraltar (1829), Bermuda (1834), Tasmania (1838), Bombay (1846), Canada (1852), South Africa (1858) and New Zealand (1871).

Ironically England was also responsible for the building in 1816 of America's first unmistakable yacht, that is to say the first boat built in America exclusively for pleasure. Certainly yachts existed in America before 1816 but the usual difficulty arises in distinguishing them from the crowd of workboats, whereas with George Crowninshield's *Cleopatra's Barge,* launched in November of that year, there can be no doubt but that she was exclusively built for pleasure. The fact that there was little time for pleasure, while the new American Republic struggled for a foothold during those early years of the nineteenth century, makes the building of *Cleopatra's Barge* remarkable.

During the war of 1812 the Crowninshield family had run a shipping business in Salem, Massachusetts, and had engaged freely in privateering—with some success. They captured British ships and cargo and sold them in Boston for over $1,000,000. With such a fortune behind him, it is not suprising to find a few years later that George Crowninshield had decided to pull out of the shipping business in order to devote his time in the planning and building of a yacht.

Cleopatra's Barge was built in Salem by Becket's shipyard and no expense was spared in her outfitting. She was 100 ft. long overall on a beam of 23 ft. and with a draught of 11½ ft. Her foremast was square rigged with fore- and aft-rigging employed on the rear two masts. Her sails and gear were of the best quality. The main saloon measured 20 sq. ft. and the interior furnishings were lavish, every item down to the cutlery being specially commissioned.

The reputed cost of this amazing vessel, in 1816, was $50,000. Had Charles II been so free with English gold, then Samuel Pepys would have turned white with horror at his desk in the Admiralty.

In 1817, George Crowninshield set off for a Mediterranean cruise with fourteen guests aboard *Cleopatra's Barge*. On 18th April they reached the Azores and progressed via Gibraltar, Tangier and Majorca to Spain and Italy. Whenever she reached port the *Barge* attracted a horde of astonished sightseers. It was remarkable in those days to see an American at all, and this superb yacht must have given countless Spaniards and Italians an inaccurate picture of life in the New Republic. As for George Crowninshield, he was delighted to be the centre of so much attention and tireless in his efforts to show people round his new home. Eight thousand people visited the *Barge* in one day in Barcelona. A carving of an American Indian stood on deck in full war paint and was the object of great curiosity. A Frenchman saluted this strange figure while some Italian visitors, believing it to be an American saint, kissed its feet.

Cleopatra's Barge reached home in October of 1817 and the owner, glowing with his success in Europe, set about laying plans for a similar voyage to England and the Baltic. Unfortunately he died before a start could be made and the *Barge* became a merchant ship although she was curiously unsuited for this service. King Kamehameha II of the Sandwich Islands (Hawaii) purchased her in 1820 but drove her on to a reef shortly afterwards.

Mr Weld's **Lulworth** (left) entering Portsmouth Harbour. She was one of the three great competitors in the racing season of 1829, but she lost the King's Cup to Lord Belfast's Louisa after the two yachts had collided within sight of the finish line.

The Royal Yacht, **Mary** (flying the Royal Standard), under storm canvas. The vessel in the foreground is in some difficulty. It is recorded that the same storm laid Mary on her beam ends.

The brief, glorious and almost priceless career of *Cleopatra's Barge* provided the singular yachting event in America during the early nineteenth century. Her appearance did turn the minds of the hard working, new Americans who lived on the eastern seaboard towards the idea of boating for pleasure. But it would not be true to say that she triggered off a yachting craze. Although isolated boats, qualifying as yachts, sailed the waters around New York and Boston during the twenties and thirties America, unlike England, had yet to produce a leisure class.

By 1820 the English leisure class were throwing themselves into yachting with vigour. Cowes began to rival Brighton as a fashionable seaside resort and the Solent rapidly became a yachtsman's playground. Members of the Royal Yacht Club were not only well-born but rich and they began building and racing yachts in earnest. Great vessels like the *Menai* and *Miranda* cost their owners £8,000 apiece, while the 120 tonner *Lulworth* left Mr Joseph Weld little change out of £14,000, a huge sum for those times. Lord Yarborough's full-rigged ship, *Falcon* (351 tons) was not unlike a twenty-gun ship of war. Certainly she sailed under the strict discipline of a man-of-war. Her Captain was a naval lieutenant and she was manned by a crew of fifty-four 'choice hands', who voluntarily placed themselves under the martial discipline of the times. A visitor aboard *Falcon* in the first year of her career wrote: 'The honest tars are so convinced of the impossibility of being properly managed without due sense of the cat-o'nine-tails that they voluntarily consented to its lawful application on board.'

The majority of yachts of the Royal Yacht Club carried brass guns and an armoury of rifles and cutlasses. The cannon were used for firing salutes and the cutlasses were particularly useful for cutting away the rigging when two yachts ran foul of each other, for races were desperately contested, and with several thousand guineas at stake some of them were literally fought to a finish.

One of the most exciting of these early races was that sailed between Mr Assheton-Smith's *Menai*, Lord Belfast's *Louisa* and Mr Weld's *Lulworth* in the summer of 1829. They had raced against one another before and their rivalry had spread to the crews, who were not always under perfect control. Lord Belfast had defeated the other two, racing in a regatta at Southampton, and he was determined to beat them again in the race for the King's Cup at Cowes. This race was run in a light breeze and on the return leg *Lulworth* and *Louisa* sailed back through the Solent together, separated by a few seconds as they rounded the markboat off Yarmouth. As they neared Cowes the two boats came into collision, whereupon *Louisa*'s crew drew their cutlasses and knives and cut away the earing of *Lulworth*'s boom as well as her reef pendant, leaving her disabled. Because of the light wind, the race had been a slow one and this collision took place late at night when the roads were ablaze with fireworks, let off in honour of the King's birthday. In the midst of this display and while the yachts anchored in the roads were firing their cannons, the crews of *Louisa* and *Lulworth* were fighting like pirates.

Mr Weld lodged a protest against Lord Belfast but the stewards of the club decided in the latter's favour, adding that they were of the opinion that 'the use of axes in the cutting away of rigging was unjustified'. Tempers still ran high and when the yachts met at Portsmouth a few days later, *Louisa* ran into *Menai*.

As a result of these disputes, Mr Assheton-Smith announced that in future he was determined to take his aquatic excursions in a steam vessel of extraordinary size. This he proceeded to do, commissioning a series of nine such craft between 1830 and 1851. Steam yachting was regarded as ungentlemanly and its pioneer was therefore treated with suspicion, but Mr Assheton-Smith was undeterred. He simply resigned from the Royal Yacht Club and steamed away. Mr Weld was more tenacious and, refusing to be intimidated by the ferocity of Lord Belfast, spent a fortune on new racing yachts during the next two years without any success.

Lord Belfast was the most remarkable yachtsman of the age. After three unbeaten years with *Louisa* he could boast that he had proved to the world that he owned the fastest cutter afloat. Adding that he would now see what he could do with a square-rigger, he built the brig *Waterwitch,* whose speed was destined to alter the design of ships of the entire Royal Navy. In 1833, determined to prove the superiority of his new brig, Lord Belfast challenged Mr C. H. M. Talbot's schooner *Galatea* to a race from the Nab round the Eddystone Lighthouse and back, a distance of 224 miles, the first ocean race ever sailed. *Waterwitch* emerged the winner by twenty-five minutes, her opponent having lost her jib-boom and topmast in heavy weather on the homeward run. £50,000 changed hands as a result of this match.

After this success Lord Belfast made a habit of lying in wait for any man-o'-war leaving Portsmouth Harbour, in order that he might outsail them. Sometimes, just to rub it in, he would order sail to be shortened and still leave the King's ships far astern. He did this so often and with such outstanding success that in 1834 the Admiralty bought *Waterwitch*, to use her as a trial horse against the ships of their Fleet.

It was through the offices of Lord Belfast and in recognition of the Royal Yacht Club's service to the Navy that William IV granted permission for it to be styled the Royal Yacht Squadron, with himself as Admiral. From then until the present day, except in times of war, yachts belonging to members of the Squadron have been privileged to fly the White Ensign when the owner is on board.

By the middle of the nineteenth century British yachtsmen considered themselves superior to all others, their great schooners, cutters and brigs flying like giant butterflies over the summer seas. But by now there were signs that yachtsmen in America were beginning to organize themselves.

John Cox Stevens, a contemporary of Lord Belfast, has been called the father of American Yachting. His family lived on the Hudson River across from New York where small boat sailing for pleasure proved increasingly popular during the 1830s and 1840s. A variety of craft were used for this purpose but the most common type was known as a sandbagger.

Lord Belfast's brig **Waterwitch** leading Mr Talbot's schooner **Galatea** at the start of the first ocean race ever held. The prize for the contest was £1,000, and the course lay from the Nab round the Eddystone lighthouse and back, a distance of over 200 miles. Betting was heavy, and over £50,000 changed hands as a result of Waterwitch's victory.

The sandbagger was directly related to local fishing craft and measured between 20 and 30 ft. long. It carried a huge, sloop-rigged sail area on a shallow, wide beam, centreboard hull which was ballasted with sandbags. There was a constant danger of capsizing but the crews of these boats, made up of New York longshoremen and other waterfront characters, raced their sandbaggers hard and fearlessly.

John C. Stevens owned a string of boats, starting when he was 24, and it is likely that his enthusiasm for yacht racing was founded in a sandbagger or in a similar type of vessel. By 1844 he owned a fast 51-ft. schooner called *Gimcrack*, designed by George Steers. It was on board this yacht that Stevens held the inaugural meeting of the New York Yacht Club, at 5.30 p.m. on 30th July 1844. Prominent New Yorkers who attended this meeting and who became founder members of the club were Louis Augustus Depau, John Jay, George Schuyler, Captain James Rogers, James Waterbury, George Rollins, Hamilton Wilkes and William Edgar.

In the following year (17th July 1845) the New York Yacht Club sponsored America's first formal yacht race. William Edgar's *Cygnet* won the cash prize of $225 and *Gimcrack* came third. John Stevens could hardly be satisfied with this result, so he promoted a design and building programme to be carried out by his confederates which proved comparable to that undertaken amongst members of England's Royal Yacht Club, little more than a decade earlier. John Stevens played the part of Lord Belfast, making up for his lack of ferocity in that role by his development of advanced design techniques. Together with his brother Edwin, he commissioned a new sloop called *Maria*. This yacht measured 110 ft. overall, 26½ ft. in the beam on a draught of 5 ft. (with the centreboard hoisted). In order to keep down the weight, Stevens invented hollow masts and booms to carry her huge sail area. The sails were sewn parallel to the boom, where before they had been sewn vertically, thus decreasing the wind resistance of the seams. She had no difficulty in winning her first race in 1846 and

Stevens had good reason to claim that in *Maria* he owned the fastest yacht in New York harbour.

Gigantic centreboarders, carrying extravagant sail areas like *Maria*, were designed to make the best of local conditions. New York waters were extensive and sheltered but they were shallow. John Stevens and his friends, having 'got their eye in' with centreboarders, began to feel that it was time for America to take on the English yachtsmen, who by now were convinced of their superiority in the sport. Clearly they would have to build a new boat, capable of crossing the Atlantic and more suitable for racing in deeper English waters. For this purpose a syndicate was formed in New York Yacht Club, with Stevens and George Schuyler at its head, and George Steers was engaged to design a schooner based on New York pilot boat lines.

In due course the new schooner, named *America*, was delivered and on 31st July 1851 she set sail for England where she was to win the trophy now known as the America's Cup and where she was to assume the mantle of superiority in the sport of yacht racing which the United States still wears today. But in spite of *America*'s victory in 1851, the growth of yachting during the nineteenth century continued to be led, unmistakably by England.

Australia, amongst the British colonies, was slow to start yachting although worth some mention here because in the 1950s and 1960s she was to emerge as the first serious challenger to American and British yachting supremacy. The first white settlement in Australia had been established in Sydney cove as early as 1788, thirteen years after the founding of the Cumberland Fleet. It was not until 1827, however, that there is any record of organized yachting in that country. A regatta was held in Sydney Harbour during the summer of 1827 in which six yachts took part. The regatta was a success and became an annual event. By 1842 it was an attractive enough event to draw a crowd of 10,000 spectators.

But in many ways Australia was in a similar situation to America in that she suffered the growing pains of a new country and it was not until the second half of the nineteenth century that Australians found much time for yachting. By 1860 the population exceeded a million and there was more time and money available for leisure.

Although the Royal Sydney Yacht Club was founded in 1862, it was not until the 1880s and 1890s that Australian racing yachts were subjected to the sophisticated kind of design development that Lord Belfast in England and John Stevens in America had pioneered over fifty years earlier. It is interesting to note that the leading Australian designer of the day, Walter Reeks, was sent to America and England in 1888 by a syndicate of Sydney yachtsmen to obtain information relating to a challenge for the America's Cup. Sufficient funds were not forthcoming and the project lapsed for over seventy years.

By the end of the nineteenth century, the sport was established throughout the world. In addition to those mentioned already, early yacht clubs had been established in France (1838), Belgium (1847), Portugal (1856), Sweden (1860), Finland (1861), Germany (1868), Spain (1879) and Italy (1879). The first yacht club in South America was founded in Argentina in 1883.

With the launching of the schooner *America*, the difficulty which confronts yachting historians ceases to exist. From 1851 the sport developed steadily, with Anglo-American rivalry as a driving force, but the initial problem still remains unsolved: when did yachting start? Did it all begin on the Nile in 1500 B.C. or on the Dutch rivers in the seventeenth century? Did Charles II or the Duke of Cumberland found modern yachting, or were the members of the Water Club of the Harbour of Cork the real founders? There is no satisfactory answer to these questions. Pleasure boats have existed from the earliest times and to say, for instance, that the Dutch or the Duke of Cumberland invented yachting would be incorrect. It would be incorrect to say that John Stevens was America's first yachtsman because he was preceded by George Crowninshield, the owner of *Cleopatra's Barge*. Yet after the Duke of Cumberland had founded the Cumberland Fleet in 1775 we can trace the progress of yachting in England along a steady course. In America the same can be said during the years following the foundation of the New York Yacht Club in 1844. These two incidents mark the turning points in history where the sport became an organized rather than a haphazard activity. After a series of fits and starts, it was these two incidents which presaged a world-wide growth in the popularity of yachting.

The America's Cup

THE AMERICA'S CUP HAS BECOME THE PRESTIGE EVENT ON THE YACHTING CALENDAR. THE aura of unattainability which surrounds this famous trophy has contributed more, perhaps, to its current status than any other single factor. American yachtsmen won the trophy from Great Britain in 1851 and twenty attempts have been made to take it off them since then. Many of these challenges have afforded excitement but only three of them have come close to success: those of the cutter *Shamrock IV* in 1920, the J class *Endeavour* in 1934 and the Australian 12 Metre *Gretel* in 1962. Each of their respective opponents, *Resolute, Rainbow* and *Weatherly* were stretched to the limit in defence of the Cup.

The history of America's Cup competition can be divided into three phases. The initial phase extended from that first American victory in 1851 up to 1899. During this period contests for the Cup were conducted under conditions and regulations which British yachtsmen considered, with some reason, were balanced in favour of the American defenders. The disputes and the acrimony which resulted from this state of affairs reduced the competition to its lowest level.

The golden age of the America's Cup began in 1899 and continued up to the Second World War. During this period the spirit of competition was rekindled by Sir Thomas Lipton, with a determination, sportsmanship and financial expenditure that have become legendry. Between 1899 and 1930, this self-made man challenged five times for the America's Cup unsuccessfully, earning praise from his opponents as 'the world's best loser'. Lipton's challenges set a relentless pace for the development of the racing yacht, to be followed by designers on both sides of the Atlantic—Herreshoff, Burgess and Stephens in America and Fife, Watson and Nicholson in England. The climax of this design race was reached in England in 1934, after Lipton's death, when Charles Nicholson designed *Endeavour* for Sir T. O. M. Sopwith's first challenge for the Cup. In America the climax came in 1937 with the joint Burgess/Olin Stephens design, *Ranger*. The current esteem which the contest enjoys was earned largely by Sir Thomas Lipton and Sir T. O. M. Sopwith, together with their opposing American defenders, Iselin, Morgan, Rockefeller and Vanderbilt.

The era of the giant cutters and the J class yachts died with the war and America's Cup history entered its third phase in the 1950s when serious efforts were made to open up the competition. Sensible alterations to the rules which govern the event, and a reduction in the size of America's Cup yachts, combined with the acceptance of a challenge from Australia, has ended the old closed-shop tradition. Today, 12 Metre tongues are licking their lips in Greece, Italy and France as well as in Britain and Australia, all thirsting for a successful draught from the America's Cup.

The trophy is named after the schooner *America* which was designed by George Steers and built in 1851 at William H. Brown's shipyard in New York. 101 ft. overall, she was 90 ft. on the waterline, 23 ft. in beam with a draught of 11 ft. These dimensions indicated design thinking in America which was very different from the persistent English practice of constructing narrow beamed hulls which depended on much deeper and heavily weighted

Driven hard, a **12 metre** carves through a good lop during America's Cup trials off Newport. There are no guard rails on these boats so the crews must have the agility of a cat to stay aboard, combined with the strength of a gorilla to work the 'coffee grinder' winches.

12
US 17

(left) **Weatherly** crosses **Gretel's** bow. It was these magnificent short tacking duels that were the feature of the Australian challenge of 1962.

(right) The latest Australian challenger for the 1970 America's Cup series, **Gretel II.** The competition has been opened up in the last few years with a number of European countries, apart from England, showing interest in making a challenge. Challengers in future should stand a better chance of winning the trophy now that they can be tested in pre-series elimination trials between themselves.

(on next two pages) Australia's moment of triumph. **Gretel** surges past **Weatherly** to take the lead in the magnificent second race of the 1962 series. The Australian boat always seemed the faster on spinnaker reach if there was a stiff enough breeze.

keels for stability—the 'plank-on-edge' concept. By British standards *America* was also revolutionary in rigging. She carried over 5,000 sq. ft. of sail on two sharply raked masts and both her main and fore-sails were laced to booms. All the sails were made of machined cotton which enabled them to set much flatter than the baggy flax sails of the British yachts.

America was owned by a syndicate of American yachtsmen headed by Commodore John C. Stevens. She sailed across the Atlantic and was refitted at Le Havre before crossing the channel to Cowes. Off the Needles the British cutter *Laverock* lured her into a test of speed and was decisively beaten. As a result no one offered to give Stephens a race for several weeks. Finally the Royal Yacht Squadron invited *America* to take on fourteen British yachts in a race round the Isle of Wight for the 'One Hundred Guinea Cup'. Thus Stevens was forced into competition in confined waters without benefit of local knowledge of tides and sand-banks or of the usual time-allowance or handicap, but since it was all he was offered he had to accept. The race took place on 22nd August 1851 and is described by the designer's nephew, Henry Steers, who sailed aboard *America*:

> The wind was from the westward. The yachts were allowed to get up their sails after the first gun, but we found that we constantly overran our anchor and slewed round, and we had to lower our sails; and so all the yachts got off ahead of us; however, we had a very large crew and got our sails up very quickly. By the time we got to the Nab (12 miles) we had walked through the whole fleet except four (*Beatrice*, *Aurora*, *Volante* and *Arrow*). We were running wing to wing, and these boats would steer close together, so that when we tried to get through them we could not without fouling, and had to keep cutting and sheering about, very often being near gybing. From the Nab to St Catherine's the wind was ahead and there we left them so fast that when we got down to the Point there was not a yacht in sight. Here we caught the tide, and the little *Aurora* came up pretty near to us, and the *Arrow* was just behind her. After getting to St Catherine's Point we had a leading wind and we went there to the Needles at the rate of thirteen or fourteen knots. . . . We arrived at Cowes about eight o'clock.

At the first and only attempt, in adverse and unfair conditions, *America* had trounced the cream of the British fleet. In so doing the Americans established a design superiority which they have never really lost.

Commodore Stevens took the 'One Hundred Guinea Cup' home with him to New York and six years later the syndicate presented it to the New York Yacht Club as an international challenge cup to promote 'friendly competition between countries'. The letter outlined what appeared to be straightforward details of competition.

> Sir: The undersigned, members of the New York Yacht Club, and the owners of the schooner yacht, *America*, beg leave through you to present to the Club the Cup won by the *America*, at the Regatta of the Royal Yacht Squadron, at Cowes, England, on 22nd August 1851. . . .
>
> The Cup is offered to the New York Yacht Club subject to the following conditions:
>
> Any organized yacht club, of any foreign country, shall be entitled through any one or more of its members, to claim the right of sailing a match for the Cup with any yacht or vessel of not less than 30 or more than 300 tons, measured by the Custom House Rule of the country to which the vessel belongs.
>
> The parties desiring to sail for the Cup may make any match with the yacht club in possession of the same that may be determined upon by mutual consent: but in the case of a disagreement as to terms, the match shall be sailed over the usual course for the Annual Regatta of the yacht club in possession of the Cup, and subject to its Rules and Sailing Regulations. . . .
>
> The challenging party being bound to give six months notice in writing, fixing the day they wish to start. This notice to embrace the length (Custom House Measurement) and the name of the vessel.
>
> It is to be distinctly understood that the Cup is to be the property of the Club, and not of the members thereof or the owners of the vessel winning the match, and that the conditions

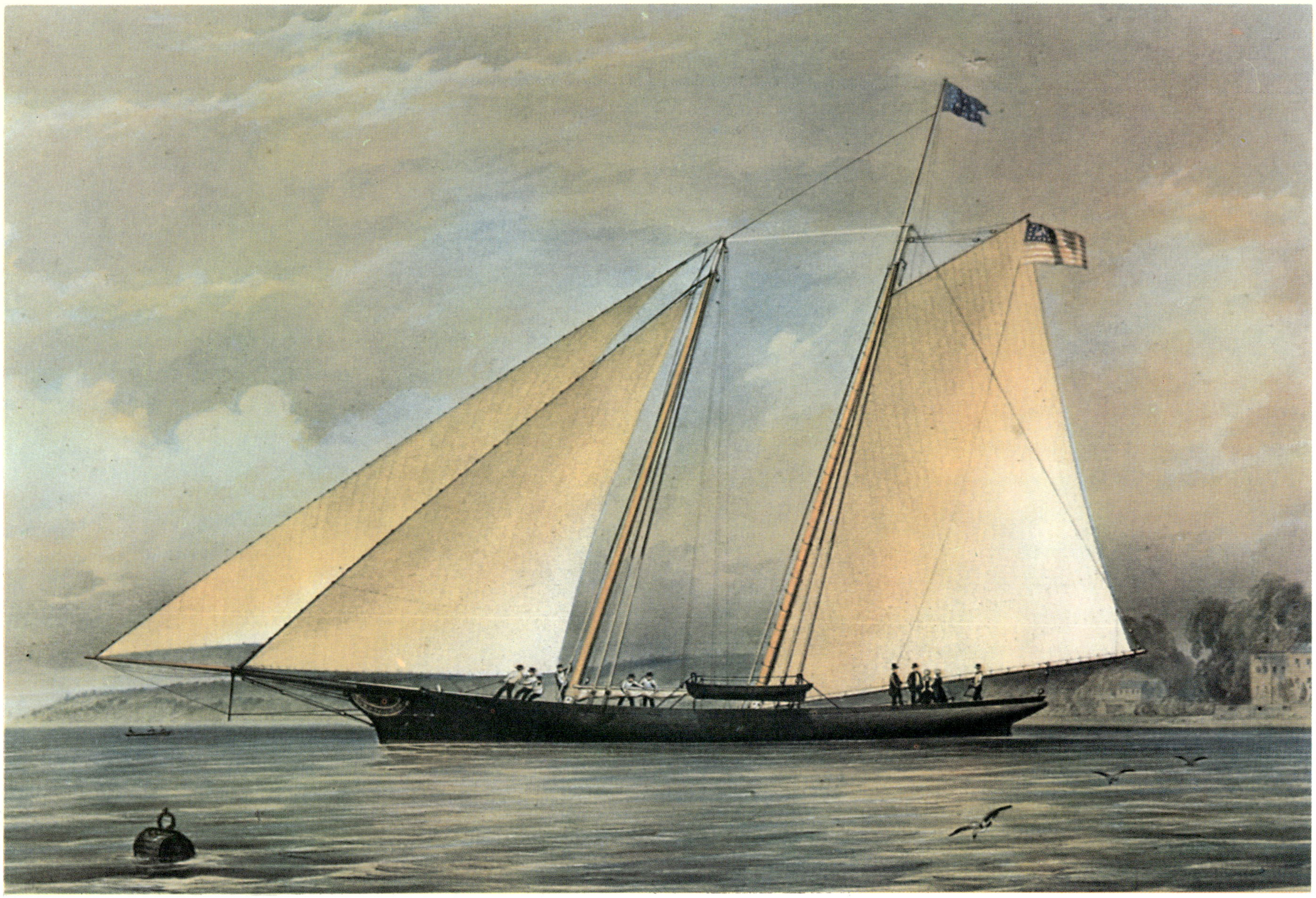

The **America** was designed by George Steers for a syndicate of American yachtsmen, headed by the father of American yachting, Commodore John C. Stevens. Her lines were basically those of a New York pilot boat, and startled British yachtsmen, whose yachts were built on a much narrower beam and depended on deeper, heavier keels for stability. Note the sharp angle of rake to the masts, and the fact that her main and fore sails are laced to booms.

of keeping it open to be sailed for by yacht clubs of all foreign countries, upon the terms above laid down, shall forever attach to it, thus making it perpetually a Challenge Cup for friendly competition between countries.

Perhaps the Cup was infected with the reluctance shown by British yachtsmen to give *America* a fair race, for few of the early challenges were carried out in the spirit of friendly competition outlined in the Deed of Gift. In 1870, at the first challenge, there was argument over whether the challenger should race against one selected defender or against a whole fleet as *America* had had to do at Cowes, and James Ashbury's *Cambria* raced against a fleet of seventeen. There was also dispute over the American centre-board yachts. The British claimed it was unfair that their ocean-going yacht should have to compete against what they regarded as specialized inshore 'skimming-dishes'. *Cambria* came tenth and was defeated by centre-boarders and keel boats alike.

For the second British challenge in 1871, the Americans conceded that only one yacht should defend in each race, but claimed that they could choose a different defender each day so as to make the most of the prevailing weather conditions.

The third and fourth challenges for the Cup came from Canada in 1876 and 1881. The Canadians felt that they had an advantage over British yachtsmen in that their challenging yachts would not have to make the Atlantic crossing prior to the contest. Consequently it would be possible for them to meet the Americans with a yacht of lighter, specialized construction better suited to American sailing conditions. Both these Canadian challenges

failed, largely because they were not backed with sufficient experience of deep water sailing and because the Canadian yachts could not be equipped with top-class gear through lack of funds.

In 1885 the Deed of Gift was amended. The Americans conceded that only one yacht could be selected to defend each challenge. But at the same time they put three new safety lines round the Cup: first, that if a yacht was defeated in a challenge it could not challenge again for two years; second, that the challenger had to cross the Atlantic on her own bottom (this had always been the case, in practice, but the new rule enforced it); and third, that challenges had to be issued ten months in advance together with the proposed dimensions of the challenger. The advantage of the last clause for the Americans was that they could now build as many potential defenders as they wished, with the dimensions of the challenger in mind, and then choose the best of them.

The schooner yacht **America** came to England in 1851 and won the trophy which is now known as the America's Cup. One of the all-time greats, it is fitting that the world's premier yachting contest should be named after her.

Valkyrie II was designed in 1893 for the Earl of Dunraven and marked the incorporation of American design techniques in a British yacht.

Under the new rules the next three challengers were quite ineffectual although they were at least amiable. Then, in 1893 the British designer, G. L. Watson, produced *Valkyrie II* for the Earl of Dunraven. Watson had assimilated some of the techniques of American yacht design and constructed a much beamier hull with a steel frame for the new challenger. Lord Dunraven came closer to success than any of his predecessors with his first challenge. Unfortunately his second challenge in 1895 gave rise to petulant accusations of cheating, protests, fouls and disqualifications. Fortunately for America's Cup yachting a new challenger came forward in 1899 to revive enthusiasm for the competition, which might otherwise have remained buried forever beneath the ill-feeling created between British and American yachtsmen by the 'Dunraven affair'.

The challenge of 1899 was made under the flag of the Royal Ulster Yacht Club by Thomas Lipton, who had built up an enormous grocery empire and who owned a large steam yacht

Shamrock IV (leading the American defender **Resolute**) came closer to taking the America's Cup off the Americans than any other challenger either before or after the series in 1920.

but whose experience of racing under sail was limited. If Lipton lacked this specific experience he made up for it by applying both his business acumen and his considerable financial resources to the task of winning back the America's Cup.

For the first time both the challenger and the defender for the 1899 series were constructed specially for the event regardless of cost. Lipton's *Shamrock* was designed by William Fife and her opponent, *Columbia,* by Nat Herreshoff. Both were designed to give their best performance under the light wind conditions which prevailed in American waters. In this respect both yachts featured extensive overhang fore and aft and carried a large spread of canvas, the principle being that as the yacht heeled over a large area of her overhanging hull came into contact with the water and her waterline length increased. The speed through the water of any displacement yacht is directly linked to her waterline length. There was very little to choose between the design of the two yachts, which both carried in excess of 13,000 sq. ft. of canvas. But *Columbia* may have held a slight advantage in that she won the overhang stakes by three feet (she measured 131 ft. overall as opposed to *Shamrock*'s 128 ft. overall, both on an 89 ft. waterline length). However, the Americans defeated Lipton's first challenge largely through the greater expertise of Charlie Barr, *Columbia*'s skipper. Ignoring this fact Lipton concentrated on the design aspect of his next challenger, *Shamrock II.*

Shamrock II, designed by G. L. Watson, probably had the edge in performance on *Columbia,*

In **Shamrock IV** the designer Charles Nicholson produced a unique yacht. Her construction was the lightest of any of the mammoth cutters, her appearance the ugliest. Note the very short bowsprit and the blunt bowline.

which defended the Cup for the second time in 1901, again with Charlie Barr as her skipper. This time there was no doubt that Lipton's second challenge was beaten by the way in which the Americans handled their boat and the racing tactics which they employed. Lipton's third challenge in 1903 was defeated by a triumph of American design, when his *Shamrock III* was trounced by *Reliance*, designed by Nat Herreshoff and carrying the overhang principle to its extreme (144 ft. overall on a 90 ft. waterline), with 2,000 sq. ft. of sail in excess of her opponent and a revolutionary steel mast. Thus Sir Thomas Lipton has been beaten twice by superior American tactics and once by superior design, now he took a ten-year 'breather' and gathered strength for his major assault.

Shamrock IV was designed and built in 1913 by Charles Nicholson, the last and lightest of the giant cutters to challenge for the Cup. Her wide space-frame construction of navaltum and laminated wood supported multiple spruce stringers and her triple-skinned planking was of laminated cedar, spruce and mahogany. With her snub-nosed bow and her chopped-off stern, with her curved 'tumble-home' sides and hogged sheer, the brilliantly designed *Shamrock IV* was known as the 'Ugly Duckling'.

The Great War forced Lipton to postpone his new challenge with *Shamrock IV* until 1920, when the defender was *Resolute*, also built in 1913 and the last big yacht to be designed by Nat Herreshoff. Each had an amateur helmsman for the first time—Sir William Burton in *Shamrock* IV and Charles Adams, the Secretary of the U.S. Navy, in *Resolute*. *Shamrock IV* was a larger boat and so conceded several minutes in time allowance, but she had an easy victory in the first race when *Resolute* broke her main gaff.

The second race was held in variable conditions which tested the yachts' performance and the result was much more encouraging to the challengers. Burton made a good start and steadily increased his lead to win by 9 minutes—$2\frac{1}{2}$ corrected.

Shamrock only needed to win the third race to take the Cup. Over the windward course *Resolute* drew ahead by two minutes, but on the run home under spinnakers *Shamrock IV* overhauled to such good effect that many Americans thought the Cup had gone at last. *Shamrock IV* crossed the line ahead but failed to make up the time allowance and the race went to *Resolute*.

Shamrock IV had shown her best performance in a good breeze and when the morning of the fourth race brought a strong wind she came out with a double-reef in her main and a

(right) The British challenger in 1934 was **Endeavour**, probably the greatest of Charles Nicholson's designs.

(below) The defender in 1920 was **Resolute**, designed by Nat Herreshoff. She held an advantage over Shamrock IV to windward, attributable perhaps to the definite V shape of her forward hull section.

J
K 4

small jib and topsail. But *Resolute* had no reefing facilities so the Race Committee first postponed the start and then cancelled the race for the day. When it was eventually held in lighter conditions it went easily to *Resolute* leaving the series all square.

Sir Thomas and Lady Sopwith at the helm of **Endeavour**.

Everything depended on the last race, which again was run under light and flukey conditions. Nevertheless, *Shamrock IV* began to work ahead until Burton decided to hold his course in search of more wind off the New Jersey shore. Adams stood out to sea and the yachts parted company. When they came together again at the finish Adams' decision was seen to have been the right one and *Resolute* won the race and the series.

Lipton's fourth challenge had been the closest in the history of the Cup and a fitting swansong for the giant gaff-rigged cutters which had dominated the competition. Once again there had been little to choose between the two yachts for performance. In most respects *Shamrock IV* held the advantage except when sailing to windward, here *Resolute*'s superiority may have been due to the definite and revolutionary *V* shape of her forward hull section (as opposed to the more traditional rounded formation employed for *Shamrock*). It is likely that *Shamrock IV* lost any advantage she may have held in performance by having to give away a little on time allowance to her opponent. There is no doubt that Sir William Burton handled *Shamrock* brilliantly throughout the series and that Sir Thomas Lipton's greatest challenge was defeated by the one factor in the competition for which he could not plan, the element of luck. If the fourth race had not been cancelled in conditions that were ideal

The crew of **Endeavour** was an almost entirely amateur one, and was formed to take the place of the original professionals after an unfortunate pay dispute. They raced against a professional Scandinavian crew aboard Rainbow and were unlucky indeed not to bring the Cup back to England in 1934.

for *Shamrock* because *Resolute* lacked reefing facilities, or if Burton had found that wind off the New Jersey shore, and his decision to search for it was unlucky but not incompetent, then it is probable that Britain would have won the America's Cup.

No new challenge was issued for the next ten years. In that time yacht design developed apace and the Bermudian rig was perfected. The rules for the America's Cup had to be changed to meet these developments. A common rating rule—the Universal—was adopted in Britain and America so that in future the competing yachts would be of the same class—the famous J class—and the time allowance was eliminated. As a measure against the temptation to build boats of dangerously light construction, Lloyds specifications were invoked and this did something to reduce the disadvantages of the challenger having to cross the Atlantic on her own bottom.

Sir Thomas Lipton was over 80 when he issued his fifth and last challenge—the first in the J class series. His new yacht, *Shamrock V*, was designed by Charles Nicholson. The Americans built no less than four J class yachts from which to choose the defender. The selected *Enterprise* was designed by Starling Burgess, who for the first time employed the new and expensive technical resources of the aircraft industry. Her light alloy mast saved over 2,000 lbs in weight and she was equipped with a highly sophisticated boom which gave some control over the curvature of the foot of the mainsail (the 'Park Avenue' boom). She completely outclassed *Shamrock V* in the 1931 series. When Sir Thomas Lipton died in the

12
KA 2

following year he was already considering another challenge. In his thirty years' participation in the competition he had lifted it from the distasteful doldrums of the Dunraven affair to its position as the most prestigeous sporting event in the world and he had set the scene for the challenge in 1934 of Sir T. O. M. Sopwith's remarkable *Endeavour*.

In every respect *Endeavour* was a masterpiece of design from Charles Nicholson's drawing-board. Her superbly shaped steel hull was of an ingenious weight-saving construction and measured 130 ft. overall on a waterline length of 83 ft. Her mast was built of steel and her aerodynamic rod rigging and tapered tubular spreaders were developed with the resources of Sopwith's aircraft organization. Nicholson evolved for her a double-clewed jib, an innovation which was poached by Starling Burgess for incorporation aboard the American defender *Rainbow*, which he had designed for a syndicate headed by Harold S. Vanderbilt.

When the two boats met for the first race in the 1934 series, Sopwith took the helm of *Endeavour* himself, in charge of an almost entirely amateur crew which had been formed to replace the original professional crew after an unfortunate pay dispute. *Rainbow* was crewed by Scandinavian professionals and steered by Vanderbilt. The time limit put an end to the first race when *Rainbow* was leading and it was re-sailed two days later over the windward and return course. The start was generously delayed to allow *Endeavour* to hoist her mainsail and on the turn *Rainbow* lead by 18 seconds. But on the run home, with spinnakers flying before a fresh breeze, *Endeavour* forged ahead to win by over 2 minutes.

The second race was run over the triangular course and Sopwith gave *Endeavour* a good start and held the advantage to the first turn. She gained more ground on the second leg but began to drop back on the broad reach home because she was making do with a small jib in place of her torn genoa. *Rainbow* was gaining fast when *Endeavour* crossed the line with a lead of 51 seconds. *Endeavour* soon established a commanding lead in the third race, to round the final mark 6 minutes in advance of her opponent. Sopwith needed only to hold his course for home in order to win the America's Cup. Vanderbilt, convinced that he had lost, handed the wheel to Sherman Hoyt. What happened next has been open to different interpretations but the most probable one is that Hoyt's mastery of *Rainbow*'s genoa won her the race. Hoyt's touch with the new sail narrowed *Endeavour*'s lead and Sopwith tacked to be on the safe side and to keep between *Rainbow* and the line, but he sailed into a calm and immediately Hoyt bore away to cross the line, the winner by 3 minutes.

The fourth race was marked by controversy. *Endeavour* started badly but made up the distance by the first turn. She was to leeward of *Rainbow* when she tacked to avoid being overhauled and *Rainbow,* as overtaking boat, should have taken avoiding action. She failed to do so and Sopwith had to bear away to avoid a collision. However he hoped to win the race outright without having to lodge a protest. When it became apparent that he could not do this he hoisted the protest flag before he crossed the line. This was in accordance with English regulations but the Race Committee refused to hear his protest because, by New York Yacht Club rules, the flag should have been raised at the time of the incident. Sopwith's nerve was shaken by this affair and the crew were wearied by extensive and probably unnecessary ballast shifting. The result was that the fifth race, held in conditions that should have suited *Endeavour*, was decisively won by *Rainbow*.

Endeavour had a good start in the last race, but *Rainbow* began to catch up and engaged in a short-tacking duel from behind which *Endeavour* won. After the turn she set too much sail and while this was being replaced *Rainbow* moved ahead. *Endeavour* caught up again with the help of her spinnaker only to fall into another trap set by the wily Sherman Hoyt. He encouraged Sopwith to try to take his wind and, while the Englishman was attempting this, Hoyt manoeuvred into the leeward position from which he was able to cross the line less than a minute ahead.

A touch of luck and a touch of Hoyt had foiled Sopwith's great challenge for the America's Cup. His second attempt in 1937 with *Endeavour II* was easily defeated and it is probable that in peak condition the first *Endeavour* would still have been the better boat. Nicholson had made her lines available to the Americans after the 1934 contest for the new purpose of tank testing and an all-out technological onslaught produced their next defender. *Ranger*, a brilliant joint design, a combination of the experience of Starling Burgess and the innovatory flair of Olin Stephens.

The second Australian challenge in 1967 with **Dame Pattie**, designed by Warwick Hood, was a disappointment. Seen here during trials with **Gretel**, Dame Pattie was beaten in four straight races by Intrepid.

The golden age of the America's Cup ended in the convulsions of the Second World War, and when the world, weary of destruction, turned again to recreation, yachtsmen found the context of the America's Cup competition entirely changed. The J class had exhausted its scope for development, as had the socio-economic structures of the countries which produced them. The New York State Supreme Court altered the Deed of Gift as follows:

1. The size of the yachts to be reduced from J class to 12 Metre.
2. The challenger need no longer cross the Atlantic on her own bottom.
3. The challenger has the right to substitute another yacht for the one named in the challenge up to one week before the start of the first race. The defender must also be named one week before the race.

In 1958 the third phase of the America's Cup began and after the British *Sceptre*'s disappointing challenge the pace was set by the Australians with *Gretel* in 1962.

When the New York Yacht Club accepted the first challenge for the America's Cup from Australia an element that had lurked covertly in the background of other prestigious sporting events was brought sharply into focus—the commercial element. Australia had grown up

(below) In the 1937 series Sopwith's **Endeavour II** (nearest the camera) was easily defeated by the brilliantly designed **Ranger**.

(right, and on next two pages) For the defence of the Cup in 1934 Starling Burgess produced **Rainbow** for a syndicate headed by Harold Vanderbilt. Rainbow's main boom was mechanically bowed by winches to increase the curve of her mainsail which thus spooned up the wind more effectively. Both these photographs give superb views of Burgess boomcraft.

J
5

since the Second World War and was hungry for overseas investment. A challenge for the America's Cup was an expensive business; and the syndicate of businessmen which backed the Australian challenge was out to demonstrate that its country was worthy of big business attention. No reasonable cost was spared.

The Syndicate was headed by Sir Frank Packer, a mass-media magnate well versed in the value and exploitation of publicity. His co-backers were the Managing Directors of Ampol Petroleum and W. D. and H. O. Wills (Australia) Pty. Ltd., W. G. Walkley and N. Foley. The whole operation was closely controlled by Sir Frank Packer from beginning to end. 12 Metre racing was a new field for Australian endeavour and Packer's first move was to provide the syndicate with some worthwhile experience. He chartered *Vim*, the old American 12 Metre in which Bus Mosbacher had given *Columbia* such an unexpected run for the right to defend the Cup against *Sceptre* in 1958.

The new challenger was named *Gretel* and she was the first 12 Metre yacht to be built in Australia. She was designed by Alan Payne and built in the Lars Halvorsen and Sons yard at Ryde on the Paramatta River, thus combining the two most successful names in Australia offshore racing. *Gretel*'s immediately distinguishing feature was her 'hogged' deck. In order to obtain the maximum mast height for performance in light airs, the deck was cambered

Weatherly was originally built for the 1958 series but lost the right to defend to Columbia. After modifications, however, she emerged to defend the Cup against Gretel in 1962.

at the base of the mast to the limit allowed by the 12 Meter formula. She emerged from behind the wall of security which surrounded her construction with these dimensions: 70 ft. overall, 45 ft. at the waterline, 12 ft. beam, 9 ft. draught and 14 ft. from the tip of the keel to the deck. She was planked in Honduras mahogany and decked in Canadian cedar finished in fibre-glass. Equipped with four-speed coffe-grinder winches and sparsely furnished, she was essentially a racing machine. The only 'extra' included in her 27 tons was the two-way radio and its re-chargeable batteries with which Sir Frank Packer maintained personal contact at all times from the tender.

Trials in Sydney Harbour and offshore proved exhaustive attempts to establish the right sail, gear and crew combinations for peak performance in a variety of conditions. The two skippers were Archie Robertson and Jock Sturrock and in the informal races between *Gretel* and *Vim* there was a constant interchange of sail, gear and crew between the two yachts. Any accurate assessment of *Gretel*'s performance was precluded by the blanket of non-communication which was held over the crew and all concerned in the project. But the trials gave the syndicate good reason to believe that they had produced at least a 'good' 12 Metre.

The American yacht **Defender** (seen here in dry dock) was the object of an unfortunate incident by Lord Dunraven in the 1895 series when she defeated his Valkyrie III. He accused her owners of altering ballast after her measurements had been taken.

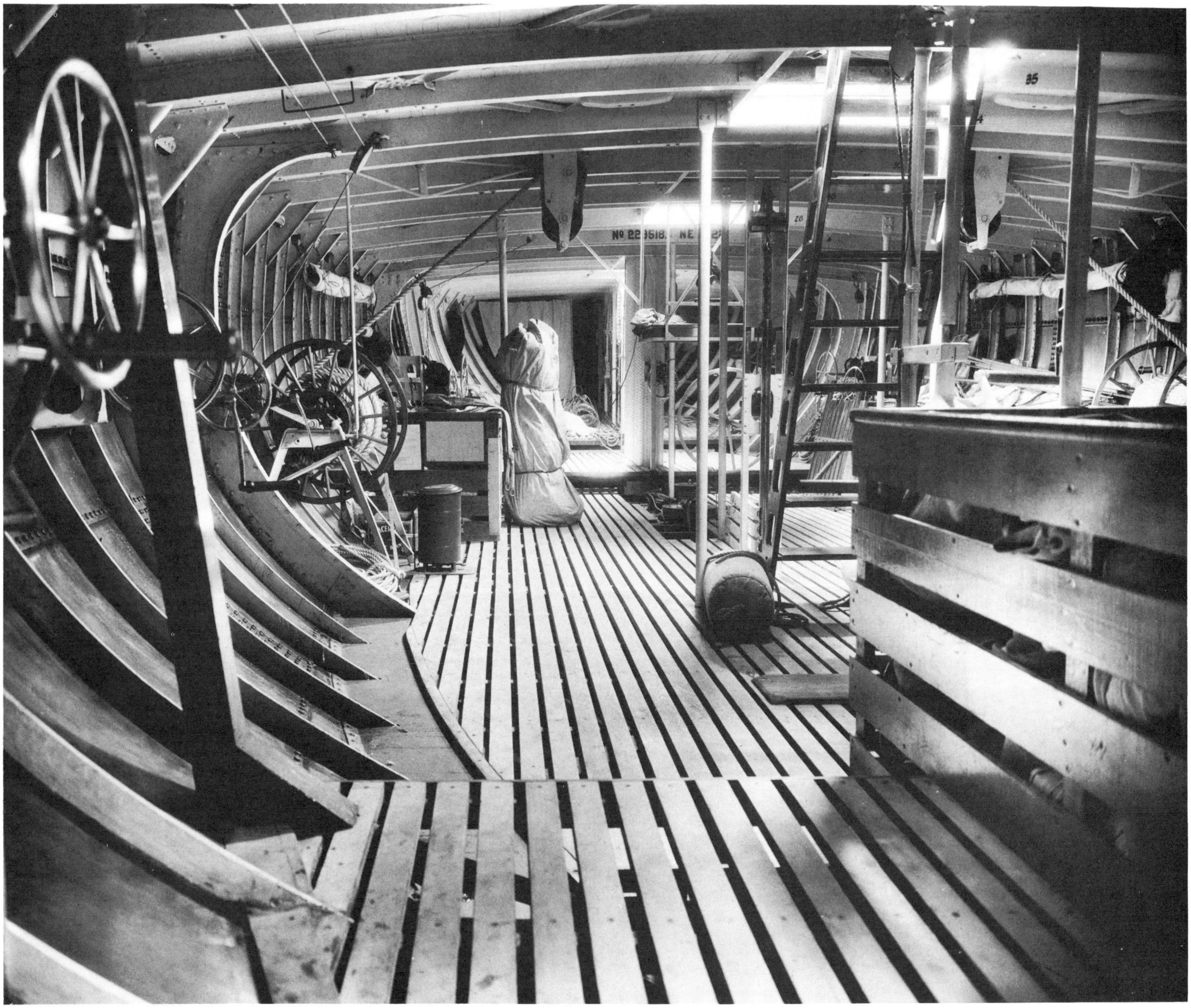

The first defender of the Cup under J class rules was **Enterprise.** The sparse layout below decks was that of an out-and-out racing machine.

Both *Gretel* and *Vim* were shipped to New York with guarded hope rather than great confidence.

Meanwhile in Newport *Weatherly*, originally built for the 1958 series but considerably improved since then, emerged as the boat to beat. Owned by a syndicate headed by Henry D. Mercer, *Weatherly* was originally a Rhodes design but her builder, A. E. (Bill) Luders of Luders Marine, was responsible for her modifications, which included re-designing her keel and cutting two feet off her stern to improve her trim. With re-positioned Ballast she sat lower in the water, but this increased stability did not detract from her light weather performance.

Once in New York the Australian party were subjected to a rigorous discipline and callisthenic training programme and installed in almost dormitory conditions at a waterside hotel. Every available moment was devoted to experimentation with new gear. The experimentation never really stopped. Only two weeks before the racing began Alan Payne had *Gretel*'s mast re-stepped 19 in. forward to correct a weather-helm. Three days before the

Enterprise annihilated Sir Thomas Lipton's last challenger Shamrock V, the most striking feature of her brilliant design being her 163ft duralumin mast which weighed only 4,000lb. A further 500lb were saved aloft by using 19-strand wires for her standing rigging and backstays. Nobody had ever seen a boom quite like the one conceived by Starling Burgess for Enterprise. Dubbed the 'Park Avenue' boom, its triangular section was fitted with frets, like a banjo, transverse slides being attached to the foot of the mainsail enabling the flow of the sail to be adjusted to suit varying wind strengths.

first race *Gretel* broke her boom in heavy weather practice and it was obvious that the Australian crew were still learning avidly under Jock Sturrock who had been appointed their skipper and helmsman for the series. In contrast the American skipper, Bus Mosbacher, was concerned with maintaining both *Weatherly* and her crew at the highest pitch of competence and confidence which they had attained during the final selection trials for the defender.

The first of the four-of-seven races was held on 15th September, after the start had been delayed for an hour while the course was cleared of a huge fleet of spectator craft. In the 18-knot wind *Weatherly* stood up well and was the stiffer boat. She pointed higher into the wind and showed she could foot faster. The wind came sufficiently out of the west to make the downwind leg a broad reach and here *Gretel* picked up 17 seconds, although she made no real impression on *Weatherly* who won by 1,200 yards—3 minutes 46 seconds. *Gretel*'s starboard backstay had parted during the race and as she rounded the final mark to start her run for home her permanent backstay had snapped. The Australians now exercised their right to a day's postponement to repair rigging.

The second race was held in heavier conditions, to which *Gretel* seemed better suited, and she showed none of the weakness to windward that had been apparent in the first race. On the triangular 24-mile course she lay 12 seconds behind at the first turn and 14 at the second. Mosbacher had the best of the start again, but Sturrock initiated a short-tacking duel from behind and halved *Weatherly*'s lead on the first leg. The fitness and training of the Australian foredeck crew paid off and it was Mosbacher who broke off the engagement as *Gretel* narrowed the distance. The last leg was decisive. In a straight run for home, *Gretel* got her spinnaker up quickly and moved up on to *Weatherly*'s weather quarter before the Americans broke out their spinnaker. This gave the Australian boat *Weatherly*'s wind and *Gretel* surged past to cross the line 47 seconds ahead. It was the first victory by a challenger since *Endeavour* had beaten *Rainbow* in 1934. *Gretel* and the Australians received a tumultuous reception for their efforts. The Australians now claimed a lay day, a major tactical error in the opinion of Bill Robinson who maintains that they missed a repetition of conditions which enabled them to win the second race and that they failed to drive home their advantage when the Americans were still badly shaken.

The wind was light and variable for the third race, which had an unusual start when the yachts crossed the line on divergent tacks. In another short-tacking duel initiated by Sturrock,

(right) **Shamrock IV**, the ugly duckling.

(below) **Ranger** leads **Endeavour II** in the 1937 series, the last J class competition.

Gretel was worsted and the wind faded to provide conditions in which *Weatherly* really excelled. Although Sturrock called two spinnaker changes *Gretel* lost distance consistently and crossed the line 8 minutes and 40 seconds behind *Weatherly*.

With the defender leading two to one in the series the fourth race was the closest in the history of the competition. *Weatherly* again took the lead from the start and in a tacking duel that was tactically mastered by Mosbacher she drew well ahead. But for the last leg the wind freshened to 10 knots and *Gretel* ran before it wearing spinnaker and staysail. She began to cut into *Weatherly*'s lead. Then the wind shifted slightly and Mosbacher immediately replaced his spinnaker with a genoa. Sturrock, with his spinnaker spilling occasionally was slow to follow suit. On the next change of wind, however, Sturrock was first up with his spinnaker and immediately began to reduce the distance, forcing Mosbacher to put out his spinnaker again. Finally, in an attempt to get to windward of *Weatherly*, Sturrock sailed into her wake and his spinnaker spilled. It was a do-or-die move and at the finish the two boats were separated only by 26 seconds.

The fifth race was the last of the series and from the start *Weatherly* drew ahead in winds that varied from 10 to 15 knots. When Sturrock tried to short-tack, Mosbacher could afford to play safe—he refused to be drawn and sailed away to a comfortable victory. The Americans retained the Cup by four to one. Jock Sturrock pointed out after the race that you learn more from losing, but in this event the Americans are just not in the habit of losing. Bus Mosbacher proved to be a professional of a different kind. In the words of his wife, he does things not for the fun of it, but to excel.

The will to win is based on experience, confidence and determination and of these the Australians lacked only specific 12 Metre experience. They extended the Americans at the first attempt and Mosbacher lost 20 lbs during the series! Even though the second Australian attempt in 1967 with *Dame Pattie* was unsuccessful, the Americans must know that their tenure of the Cup is less secure now that the Australians have the 12 Metre bit between their teeth.

The second post-war British challenge in 1964 proved disastrous when the Gubelmann syndicate defender *Constellation*, designed by Olin Stephens, thrashed Anthony Boyden's *Sovereign*, designed by David Boyd, by four races to nil. The second race in this series was won by the huge margin of 20 minutes, 24 seconds. The American success on this occasion can be attributed to a number of factors which, when compounded, proved decisive but *Constellation*'s sails were notably superior.

The direct result of the two Australian challenges was that by early 1968 interest in the America's Cup had increased and new challenges were not only under consideration in Britain and Australia but also in France and in Greece. The British and Greek challenges have not materialized but those made by Australia and France are progressing and it looks as if the next America's Cup series will be raced in 1970.

The French syndicate is headed by Baron Bisch, the manufacturer of Bic Biros, and is well advanced in the planning stage of its challenge. It has acquired a number of old 12 Metre yachts, including *Kurrewa* and *Sovereign*, to act as trial horses for a new boat. The intention is that the French and Australian challengers should both make the trip to Newport where a series of elimination trials will determine which of the two yachts should race for the Cup.

One of the most pressing disadvantages for past challengers has been their lack of competition prior to the contest. The new concept of accepting more than one challenge at a time with a view to the eventual challenger emerging from pre-series trials between the various challenging yachts may do much to keep alive the important but increasingly expensive America's Cup competition. A procedure of this kind is likely to produce a better tried and a higher calibre of challenger, with subsequently better racing.

In analysis it appears likely that the status of the trophy will remain intact whether or not the Americans continue to win it year in and year out. So long as they win, it retains that aura of unattainability which provides an almost magical spur to prospective challengers, whatever the cost. Like Mount Everest, the America's Cup has to be conquered. Should the Americans lose, then we can expect them to launch the biggest onslaught in the history of the Cup in order to win it back again. Whatever happens the America's Cup will remain the greatest event on the Yachting Calendar.

Sir Thomas Lipton's greatest challenge was made with **Shamrock IV**.

12
K16

Inshore Racing

THE EVOLUTION OF YACHT RACING IN THE FIRST HALF OF THE NINETEENTH CENTURY WAS haphazard. The sport grew piecemeal in both America and Great Britain, largely through the extravagant and ferocious enthusiasm of individual yachtsmen such as Commodore Stevens of New York and Lord Belfast. Their yachts were developed from the lines of fast and well proven workboats. The schooner *America* was based upon New York pilot boat lines, while the majority of Britich yachts carried the cutter rig employed by the host of small naval and commercial craft in service around the British coast.

By 1850 the rules governing the design of racing yachts had become outdated, while at the same time enthusiasm for the sport increased. For the second half of the nineteenth century yacht racing became increasingly chaotic through lack of control, while the character of the age worked against those who sought to introduce new rules and regulations designed to improve it.

Nowadays, of course, we exist by rules and regulations; without them we should be lost. Our object in drawing up rules and regulations for a competition is to ensure that all the competitors have a fair chance of winning. The manner of Victorian competition would nowadays seem quite extraordinary, by modern standards nineteenth-century yachtsmen led a maverick existence. In order to initiate a competition the Victorian yachtsmen or yacht club first issued a challenge. This set the scene for the match. At this stage the instigator produced his rules and regulations, designed to ensure that he would win. The challengee could not possibly agree to the odds conjured up by the challenger, for they were heavily weighted against him, so he would accept the challenge by return post, but append his own rules for the contest, under which, of course, the challenger could have no hope of success. From this position the two interested parties battled it out until they reached a satisfactory compromise. In many cases the competition was won or lost before the race was even run. An error of judgment as to advantage gained by the latest exchange of rules could cost the unwary yachtsman a victory over his opponent. The Americans handled the America's Cup regulations with expertise during the latter half of the nineteenth century. One cannot write off their methods as unsporting or unscrupulous, because they were symptomatic of yachting conduct at that time.

In their attitude to the control of yacht design, racing yachtsmen on both sides of the Atlantic were primarily concerned with speed, their common object was to build faster and faster yachts. But from the outset the American obsession for speed dominated their desire for fair play. They approached the rules with every intention, if not of breaking them, of bending them in search of that extra knot or two. The American approach was a rule cheating approach. British yachtsmen on the other hand were conservative in the extreme; speed was important to them but not so important as playing the game and keeping to the rules. Unfortunately in 1850 British yachts were designed to keep to rules drawn up in 1730.

The period of yachting history between 1850 and 1914 is largely taken up with the battle to instal some form of sane control over yacht design and to set a purposeful direction in

The British 12 metre **Sovereign**, at Cowes regatta.

King Edward VII's **Britannia**, perhaps the fastest of the first class cutters ever built. A brilliant design from the board of George Watson.

which the sport could develop. It is interesting to observe that America and Britain followed different paths during these development years and that America refused to be drawn into accepting any rules used in Europe. This independence, coupled with an overwhelming obsession with speed, a growing technology and the ability to eschew tradition in the face of innovation, which British yachtsmen could never match, enabled America to gain the lead in yacht design which she holds today.

The victory of the schooner *America* in 1851 caused British yachtsmen to panic. In their efforts to recover lost face, they designed a host of freak yachts to outwit the archaic builder's rule of 1730.

The object of a rating rule is to level out the inequalities between yachts of different dimensions and sail area. It consists of a formula evolved from the dimensions of the yacht which govern her performance (length, beam, sail area and displacement). The rule of 1730 produced a time allowance scale against builder's measurements and rated yachts in tons. It taxed beam but not draught, length of keel but not length of waterline. In order to balance huge areas of canvas without losing time allowance, long, deep and narrow hulls were designed. Steeply raked sternposts were introduced, and fore-feet were cut back, in order to achieve waterline length on a short keel. These new yachts defeated older ones because they gained huge advantages from bending the rules.

In 1875 a number of yachtsmen determined to restore fair play and to check these extremes of design. They formed the Yacht Racing Association. Their first attempt at control was outmatched by the ingenuity of the designers and a bevy of new rule-cheating freaks were launched. In 1886 comparative measurement in terms of tons was abolished. A new criterion for racing yachts was devised by Dixon Kemp and implemented by the Yacht Racing Association. A yacht's dimensions ceased to be taxed under this formula, instead her rating

The cutter **Volante**, one of the British fleet beaten by the schooner **America** in the race for the Royal Yacht Squadron Cup round the Isle of Wight in 1851.

was produced by multiplying the waterline length by the sail area and dividing the resulting figure by 6,000.

The new rule was revolutionary to conservative British yachtsmen and was met with howls of protest. They anticipated, correctly, that it would render their traditional cutters obsolete. The designers, however, set off quietly for the drawing board and prepared to set tradition by its heels, and to supersede yachts which John Chamier has described as great black-hulled, sturdy boats—built like churches to the glory of God and to last for more than one generation. They had great ferocious bowsprits made from full grown trees. Their stems were hard, uncompromising, upright pillars of oak. Their topsides were as thick as a man's arm and ringed around with bulwarks like battlements.

A number of remarkable yachts were launched in 1893, designed to the new rule. Their appearance marks a turning point in the history of yachting. Beamier and built on a shallower draught they were designed to skim over the water rather than to plough through it as the old deep-keeled yachts had done. Two of these revolutionary cutters were outstanding, *Britannia,* designed by George Watson for the Prince of Wales, and *Satanita,* designed by J. M. Soper for Mr A. D. Clarke. *Britannia* proved devastatingly fast during her first season. The highlight of the summer was the arrival at Cowes of the American cutter, *Navahoe*, one of the five first-class cutters built in America that year and designed by Nat Herreshoff. *Britannia* won twelve of the thirteen races in which the two yachts met that year. At the end of her first season, as she lay in Cowes Roads, the Royal yacht flew thirty-three prize flags.
In 1894 *Britannia* improved on her record and completely outclassed another American visitor, *Vigilant. Vigilant,* a cutter of 87 ft. waterline and carrying 12,330 sq. ft. of sail was the most advanced yacht produced by American designers. She had successfully defended the America's Cup against Lord Dunraven's *Valkyrie II* but she was thrashed by *Britannia*, sailing in British

waters. The latter won twelve of their seventeen matches. The only yacht to succeed in outsailing *Britannia* by sheer speed during the 1895 season was *Satanita* and this she did on two occasions, proving herself the fastest reaching cutter in the world.

As the nineteenth century drew to a close the great design race started in earnest. The enthusiasm for competition was fired by Anglo-American rivalry, by the America's Cup and by the skill of the designers in overcoming any new rules imposed to control them. George Watson of Glasgow was the most talented of the British designers and in designing *Britannia* he could certainly claim to be more advanced than his American counterparts. But in retrospect the American Nat Herreshoff appears to be both more revolutionary and

The first class cutter **Satanita** was the only yacht to outsail Britannia in the 1895 season.

more versatile than Watson. Herreshoff has a claim to be judged the greatest designer in the history of yachting.

The Herreshoff family first set up business as yacht builders and designers in 1864 in Bristol, Rhode Island, at the head of Narragansett Bay. Nathaniel Herreshoff had designed the first fin-keel yacht in 1890 with *Dilemma*, whose shallow hull with its long overhangs fore and aft was stabilized by a steel plate, trapezoidal in profile, with a cigar-shaped bulb of lead at its base. The following year he experimented further in producing *Gloriana*. This new yacht measured 70 ft. overall but only 45 ft. 3 in. on the waterline and was designed to the 46 ft. class under the Seawanhaka rule. *Gloriana*'s long overhangs, the bluntness of her forward sections, her lack of forefeet, her light displacement and her almost triangular underwater profile astonished yachtsmen in 1891.

In many respects Herreshoff and Watson were working along the same lines and when their new techniques were perfected in 1893, with the production of *Navahoe* and *Britannia*, Watson seemed to have won the first leg of the design race hands down. But the importance

Vigilant came over to England from America in 1894 after successfully defending the America's Cup against Lord Dunraven's Valkyrie II. She was completely outclassed by Britannia, which won twelve of their seventeen matches.

12
US 20

The **12 metre** class survives to provide the America's Cup yachts and to remind us of the scale of the pre-war circuit racing Titans. Compare the handful of Twelves afloat today with the fleet of over thirty racing in British waters alone between the wars. Large by any modern standard the 12 metre yachts were like pygmies beside the great cutters and carried one quarter of the sail area of a J class boat.

Wee Win, a ½ Rater. Measuring only 15ft on the waterline, small boats like this were the result of an effort to bring yacht racing within the reach of a wider public before the turn of the century.

of one factor underlying Herreshoff's designs for *Gloriana* and *Navahoe* was not immediately appreciated. It was the application of his skill as an engineer in their construction. The use of engineering techniques in yacht building did not seem important at the time but the lead which Herreshoff established in this field provided America with a flying start in yachting technology. *Gloriana*'s hull was light, constructed of double skin planking on composite steel frames, while her rigging combined lightness with great strength. The magazine *Yachting* said at the time, before *Gloriana*, designers had shown little engineering skill in the matter of rigging.

The focus of attention in the yachting world during these closing years of the nineteenth century fell on the great masterpieces of design, the first-class cutters built to the new measurement rules. The new rules also encouraged the design of less-imposing, less-newsworthy but cheaper classes of small yacht. Sir Edward Sullivan wrote in 1892: Yacht racing, especially in the modern cutters of 150 to 170 tons, is very expensive. . . . A modern racing yacht with a crew of 30 men may, if successful, easily knock a hole in £1,000 for racing wages alone, to say nothing of cost of spars, and sails, and gear, etc. Clearly yachting could not be a popular sport at such a price (£1,000 in 1890 can be multiplied by ten to reach a sum approximating modern values) but, as Sir Edward points out: Of course, in comparison with keeping a pack of hounds, or a deer forest, or a good grouse moor, or pheasant preserving on a very large scale, the expense of yacht racing at its worst is modest. Nevertheless, it was possible to build quite small, comparatively cheap boats under the new rating rules (i.e. 1, 15 ft. waterline length $\times$ 200 ft. sail area $\div$ 6,000 = a $\frac{1}{2}$ Rater).

This opened the sport of yacht racing to a wider public, people who could only afford pheasant preserving on a very small scale. Numerous classes of these 'little' yachts (the $\frac{1}{2}$, 1, $2\frac{1}{2}$ and 5 Raters) became established around the British coast, notably in the Solent and the Clyde. Lord Dunraven, who doubtless found his America's Cup challenges modestly expensive, remarked that in a 5 Rater, you can change clothes, boil a kettle, and, on a pinch, sleep. Of course a modern yacht, built on the 32 ft. waterline length of the 5 Rater, sleeps six or eight people in comfort.

Between these economy classes and the Big Class, rating at about 150, came a number of more respectable yachts, the 10 and 20 Raters and on to the 40 Raters, which measured about 59 ft. on the waterline. But the design race promoted by the new rating rules extended to the smallest of the new classes, where the pressure of competition to develop more efficient sails and rigging was no less exacting than in the world of the first-class cutters.

In 1895 a challenge trophy was presented by the Seawanhaka Corinthian Yacht Club of

The schooner **Westward** raced in the big class on the British regatta circuit between the wars and achieved notoriety when she was owned by playboy-financier Clarence Hatry.

Oyster Bay to spur on the development of small yacht racing through Anglo-American competition. The first contest was held between a British $\frac{1}{2}$ Rater, *Spruce IV,* and *Ethelwynn,* designed to a new American rule called the Seawanhaka rule, which used a different formula to provide a similar result to the British rating: 15 ft. waterline length + 225 sq. ft. sail area ÷ 2 = 15. The new American boats were referred to as 15 footers rather than $\frac{1}{2}$ Raters and the Seawanhaka Cup was soon established as a kind of poor man's America's Cup.

The new rating rules were also responsible indirectly for the introduction of One-Design class racing. Today, when a high proportion of all sailing craft built for cruising as well as racing belong to One-Design classes, moulded in glass reinforced plastics and produced on line production methods, it is hard to appreciate that the One-Design principle was not entirely respectable at the turn of the century. In those days the individuality of a yacht lay

(left) Designed by Fife in 1907 and originally owned by Myles B. Kennedy, **White Heather** was Shamrock's keenest rival in the 23 metre class. After the First World War she raced in the big handicap fleet under the ownership of Sir Charles Allom.

(below) **Ranger,** a good example of the American J class.

(left) The smallest of the pre-war inshore racing yachts were the 6 metres. Equally popular in America and Great Britain, they provided a rating for the Seawanhaka Trophy yachts from 1922 onwards. This photograph shows **Circe,** the 6 metre which won the Trophy for Britain in 1938 and 1939.

(right) Harold Vanderbilt's 12 metre **Vim,** delivered a body blow to British yachtsmen in 1939. In that year she crossed the Atlantic and sailed 28 races in British waters, winning 19 times. The high standard of Vim's gear was largely responsible for this success. Her wardrobe of sails was vast, and her 'coffee grinder' winches enabled the crew to handle her genoas with an efficiency and speed which confounded her rivals. The greatest 12 metre never to have raced an America's Cup series, Vim sailed in the 1958 trials to find a defender and was chartered by the Australians in 1959 as a trial horse for Gretel.

at the heart of ownership, and the idea of racing two or more yachts to a standard design did not appeal to yachtsmen.

However, even dollar millionaires began to tire of having their Herreshoff designed and built yacht of this year outclassed by the Herreshoff designed and built yacht of the next. Between the late 1890s and 1914 One-Design racing became increasingly popular, The New York Yacht Club establishing classes of 30 ft. and 50 ft. on the waterline, and even a class of 70 ft., the biggest One-Design yachts ever to be built. The fashion spread across the Atlantic and in Britain the South Coast One Design class was started in 1903 during a depression in first-class racing. The new South Coast O.D.'s were designed by Alfred Mylne and measured 73 ft. overall length. Although *The Yachtsman* described them as 'the prettiest little ships that we have seen', they met with strong prejudice through being One-Design.

12
US 15

All this activity, aimed at reducing the cost of yacht racing and consequently at increasing the sport's popularity, was prompted by the development of the big cutters. Even at this early date the new changes promised to threaten the prestige of these yachting Titans. At the same time the battle of wits between the designers and the rule-makers continued, so that the course of development in the Big Class never remained stable for long.

In 1896 and 1901 the Yacht Racing Association drew up their 'Linear' rules in order to check the extreme designs which had appeared in the spate of shallow-hulled, skimming yachts following in the wake of *Navahoe*, *Britannia* and *Satanita*. They incorporated breadth and girth of the hull in the old equation based on length and sail area. As a result sail area became less heavily taxed and the Linear rules produced deep, broad yachts, built on short waterlines and carrying vast areas of sail.

The older cutters were severely penalized under the Linear rules, but many of them were re-rigged or altered in some other way and continued to race. In 1897 the impact of the first-class cutters on yacht design began to decline, although the Big Class continued to race under handicap rules until 1936.

In 1907 the International Yacht Racing Union was formed when European Nations met to adopt the same rules of yacht measurement. Eight new classes, known as Metre Classes, were drawn up. The First International Rule differed very little from the British Linear Rule of 1901, but under it the metre yachts, built to one class, could race without time allowance. It also introduced scantling tables to control construction, eliminating extremes of lightness. It was modified in 1919 and again in 1933 and survives today as the rating system for the America's Cup 12 Metre yachts.

The most majestic of the new yachts was the 23 Metre class but too few of them were built ever to provide satisfactory class racing. Of the four 23 Metres produced before 1919, *White Heather II* was the most successful and survived to race with the Big Class after the war. The 19 Metre class was even less popular producing only four boats, none of which survived the war. Sixteen yachts, however, were constructed under 15 Metre rules, Sir Charles Allom's *Istria* and the King of Spain's *Hispania* being the most notable. Fourteen pre-war 12 Metres were built but the most popular classes proved to be the smallest ones, the 8 Metres (45 boats built) and the 6 Metres (35).

In America the Universal Rule was adopted in 1903 with the same object as the British Linear rules of discouraging the design of shallow, skimming yacht hulls. American yachts built under the Universal Rule were rated alphabetically (Universal rating=18 per cent of the length of the hull, measured at one quarter of its beam, multiplied by the square root of the sail area and divided by the cube of the displacement). The Americans found this a satisfactory method of yacht measurement and saw no reason to place themselves under the International Rule when it was produced in 1907. European yachtsmen, therefore, continued to race under a rule which was not really International and the Americans to race under a rule which was certainly not Universal.

The most significant technical development during these early years of the twentieth century was the evolution of the Bermudian rig. The new rig was evolved from design thinking amongst the smaller classes of racing yacht, reflecting the exchange of influence on design between the big cutters and the more economical, popular boats. A more advanced lugsail, in a development of its old standing version was devised by Thomas Ratsey and swept the board in the rater classes up to 5 Raters. The low-peaked gaff was replaced by a much longer yard slung from a halyard rather more than two-thirds of the yard's length from the heel, forming a continuation of the mast as nearly as possible in the same line. The mainsail was increased in height and approached the triangular in profile; but the yard, doubling the mast for about half the latter's length, added to the weight aloft and clearly invited the Bermudian rig. Although the racing success of this rig was clearly accountable to the higher aspect ratio compared with gaff rigs, this was not appreciated at the time.

The First World War brought a stop to European yachting but between 1914 and 1919 the Bermudian rig became established in the U.S.A. and with resumption of inshore class racing in Europe after the war, it quickly became the only fit rig for the racing yacht. It started by being adopted in the smaller classes and soon spread to the larger ones. All the

Mr J. R. Payne's 12 metre **Vanity** in the Solent.

12 Metres had been gaff rigged in 1913 but by 1930 none of them were and in the Big Class, to most people's disquiet, *Nyria* came out as a Bermudian cutter in 1921.

In Great Britain, after the war, racing purists continued to look to the 12, 8 and 6 Metre classes for their competition, boats which were modest in size by pre-war standards. More than thirty 12 Metres were produced between 1919 and 1939 by the three British architects Fife, Mylne and Nicholson; one was also designed in 1939 by Laurent Giles. During the same period British designers produced thirty-nine 8 Metres and no less than eighty-seven 6 Metres. Today no thoroughbred regatta racing yachts of any kind are produced, except for a handful of 12 Metres built for the America's Cup, and these numbers seem impressive, but they were small in comparison with the number of Metre yachts produced during the seven-year period leading up to 1914.

The inter-war years formed, as we can see now, a natural transition between the yachting of pre-1914 and post 1946. To build large and extremely expensive yachts for the exclusive purpose of racing around the neighbouring buoys during daylight hours was obviously extravagant. In the thirties even a 6 Metre, essentially an open dayboat, cost about £2,000 with perhaps another £1,000 to keep it in commission. Nevertheless, in the 6, 8 and 12 Metre classes the pure regatta racing yacht remained alive. Rules attempted to enforce accommodation of a minimal kind but the architects, led by the owners, treated them with the attitude of 'O God make me good, but not just yet'. Yachtsmen continued to sail in peerless racing shells, content to have thermos and sandwich racing luncheons and to live in attendant motor yachts.

12
K1

(left) **Vanity** was designed by William Fife in 1922 and joined the large 12 metre fleet sailing in British waters.

(right) America's great 6 metre, **Goose,** Olin Stephens' first masterpiece.

In 1921 the Americans formed the North American Yacht Racing Union, which adopted the International measurement rules for all yachts of 12 Metres and under. Now yachts built anywhere in the world could compete on equal terms. Arrangements were made for a series of team races between Britain and the U.S.A. in the 6 Metre class. Contests for a new cup, called the British-American Cup, were to take place alternately in England and America.

Initially the Americans lacked 6 Metre experience. Consequently they were beaten in both the 1921 series for the British-American Cup held at Cowes, and the 1922 series held at Oyster Bay. They lost again in 1923 and 1924 when, under the terms of the competition,

An **M Class** yacht, designed under the American Universal Rule.

the British won the Cup outright. With a new Cup and an agreement that the contest should be held biannually, the competition was resumed in 1928. This second Cup was won outright by the Americans and so was the third Cup, by victories in 1934, 1936, 1938 and after the war in 1949.

This was not a happy period for British yachtsmen or British designers, who lost and never regained their early mastery of the 6 Metre class. In 1932 the American 6 Metres astonished British yachtsmen with the number of headsails they carried stuffed under their foredecks. *Nancy*, for example, was equipped with six of them, excluding spinnakers, when the majority of British Sixes carried a mere two.

The American approach to the problem of designing to the unfamiliar European International Rule was typically thorough. Purchasing a British Fife-designed 6 Metre, they raced her against an American boat; then lifted her lines, reconstructed them on paper and analysed them. Before long they were employing the new technique of tank testing for the hulls, developed by Dr K. S. M. Davidson in the Stevens tank at Hoboken. Olin Stephens begin-

Gloriana from the board of Nat Herreshoff went a long way to advance design thinking behind American yachts in 1891.

ning a brilliant career, produced his famous 6 Metre *Goose,* which was the product of twelve different models tried in the Hoboken tank.

The old Seawanhaka Cup also passed to the 6 Metres in 1922 but the British eclipse in this match event was not so complete as in the British-American Cup. The Scottish 6 Metre *Coila III* won it against indifferent American competition in 1922 and successfully defended it until 1925 when she was beaten by *Lanai.* In 1938 and 1939, as the curtain came down on this kind of inshore racing, the British *Circe* did something to restore prestige by defeating *Goose* in perhaps the greatest of all the 6 Metre matches, to take the Seawanhaka Trophy.

In contrast with the 6 Metres, the 12 Metre class did not prove immediately popular with the Americans, although their adoption of 12 Metre rules encouraged an active British Fleet. *Vanity,* designed by William Fife for Mr J. R. Payne in 1922, was a typical and a successful example of the new twelves.

Vanity was built at a cost of £4,500 and measured 65 ft overall, 44 ft. on the waterline, with a beam of 12 ft. and a draught of 9 ft. Her Thames tonnage was about 35 tons and she carried 2,100 sq. ft. of sail. Her accommodation consisted of a double cabin aft, passage berth to starboard, lavatory and oilskin locker to port, a large saloon and roomy fo'c'sle for four paid hands, including a professional skipper.

British 12 Metre competition reached its peak in the late twenties. Sir T. O. M. Sopwith's *Mouette*, designed and built by Charles Nicholson, was the fastest yacht in the class, winning it in both 1928 and 1929.

During this inter-war period the Big Class, sailing under handicap rules, continued to race regularly. It presented the most spectacular scenes in British yachting and included many of the all-time greats produced by the pre-war flurry of design regulations, the cutters, schooners and the biggest of the Metre yachts. While the purists were thrashing it out with twelves, eights and sixes the Big Class sailed as a superb pageant of recent yachting history. Regular competitors included the King's famous cutter *Britannia*, rigged and re-rigged according to the latest trend; the magnificent schooner *Westward*, originally designed by Nat Herreshoff and now owned in turn by the financier Clarence Hatry and the South African millionaire T. B. F. Davis; the pre-war 23 Metre *White Heather* and a number of 23 Metres built after the war, including *Astra* and *Candida*. When the American Universal Rule was adopted by European yachtsmen for the measurement of yachts in excess of 14½ Metres in 1931, the Big Class was joined by a handful of J class yachts; *Shamrock V*, *Endeavour*, *Endeavour II* and *Valsheda*, the only J class yacht ever to be built on either side of the Atlantic which never aspired to America's Cup activities.

No yachts were built in Europe to the smaller Universal Rule classes, the K and L, rating at 65 ft. and 56 ft. compared with the 76 ft. of the J class. Nor were yachts ever built to the largest of the International Rule classes, the 14½ Metres, rating at 47·55 ft. compared with the 12 Metres 39·37 ft. As a result a curiously wide gap existed in British first-class racing between the wars, separating the biggest from the next largest class. The size of racing yachts dropped abruptly from those in the Big Class, which included the J boats, to the 12 Metres, of about one half a J boat's length, one-sixth of the displacement and spreading only one quarter of the sail area. In America this gap was filled by an active M class under the Universal Rule, producing boats of some 87 ft. overall and displacing about 42 tons, which is about one-third as long again as a 12 Metre and some 50 per cent heavier.

By 1935 the whole structure supporting the inshore regatta racing yachts had begun to crumble. On the 10th August, the last day of Cowes week in that year, the great *Britannia* sailed her final race against one other cutter, three J boats and a 23 Metre. Four days later the King's sailing master, Sir Philip Hunloke, tendered his resignation as Chairman of the Royal Yachting Association, a position that he had held for twenty-five years. The King died in January 1936 and on his orders *Britannia* was scuttled on 10th July. Peter Heaton writes in his *Yachting, a History*: She was launched from Marvin's yard at Cowes, and as she lay waiting for her launch on the slipway the foreman of the yard placed over her stern-head a garland of wild flowers. She lay moored to her familiar buoy in Cowes Roads for two days awaiting the end, just a long slim black hull, no mast or rigging, everything of value, her her gear, compass, ship's wheel, had been removed.

At midnight on 9th July Sir Philip Hunloke together with *Britannia*'s skipper and her steward set out aboard one of the two destroyers which came to tow her into the Channel, where explosives were placed in her hull. When the charge went up watchers were able to see some pieces of the yacht fly into the air, but in a matter of minutes nothing was to be seen—the entire hull had disappeared. Soon after Cowes Week in 1936 the yachts of the Big Class went to their winter quarters, never to race again in British waters. In 1937 came the last America's Cup series sailed under J class rules, when the brilliantly designed *Ranger* defeated *Endeavour II*.

The end of this great era for inshore racing came with the outbreak of the Second World War in 1939. After the war yachting of this type would be confined to the America's Cup and, in a very limited way, to the Olympic keelboat classes. The great post war boom for the sport which lay ahead would take place in the fields of offshore and dinghy racing. In the closing years of peace yachtsmen on both sides of the Atlantic played out the last act for all they were worth. Britain won the Seawanhaka Trophy with *Circe* at 6 Metre level in 1938 and 1939, but in the 12 Metre class it was America who made the grand gesture as the curtain fell.

The American 12 metre **Cottonblossom**. The 12 metre class took longer to gain popularity in America than in Britain, but superior design technique soon enabled American yachtsmen to more than make up for their slow start.

12
1

(left) Sir Thomas Sopwith's **Tomahawk** was no match for Mike Vanderbilt's **Vim** in 1939.

(right) Built in 1912, the 15 metre **Istria** was designed by Charles Nicholson for Sir Charles Allom and was the first yacht to be fitted with a Marconi topmast. Stepped inside the mainmast and supported by cross trees and stays, this device saved unnecessary weight aloft. The rig acquired its name when a yachtsman standing on Ryde pierhead asked "What are all those wires and struts at the top of Istria's mast for?" "They are part of her Marconi" came the reply, "carried so that she can signal for more whisky when supplies run out". Istria, with her new rig, won 35 prizes in 36 starts in her first season.

D
7

NYYC
5

(left) One Design class racing was gaining popularity in America before the First World War. These **New York 50's** were designed by Herreshoff in 1913.

(above) **Endeavour** was built for the America's Cup to the J class Universal Rule.

The Americans had never really entered the 12 Metre class with any great enthusiasm. However, the American yachtsman Horace Havermeyer had watched the class racing in England in 1929 and had taken back to America Tommy Sopwith's *Mouette*. Over the next decade the Americans tackled the design of 12 Metre yachts with the same determined methods they had applied to their 6 Metres in the twenties. In 1939 Mike Vanderbilt crossed the Atlantic to sail his new 12 Metre *Vim* on the British regatta circuit.

Vim, designed by Olin Stephens, started the season at Harwich and competed in 28 races in British waters, winning 19 firsts, 4 seconds and 2 thirds. This score is remarkable when you consider that Vanderbilt was racing for the first time under conditions to which he was not accustomed and against eight of Britain's crack 12 Metres, including Sopwith's *Tomahawk*.

Undoubtedly, *Vim* was revolutionary in design. Her standing rigging, for example, was made from streamlined steel rods and her mast was of duralumin. But it was probably Vanderbilt's handling of her sails that won her so many races. Whatever the reason for *Vim*'s success, she shattered the last vestiges of British mastery in the design or in the sailing of inshore racing yachts. Once again American timing was perfect as they took control of the 12 Metre class, the class which was to provide the post war America's Cup yachts.

199

Ocean Racing

THE MODERN SPORT OF OCEAN RACING, WITH ITS UNDERLYING PHILOSOPHY OF PROMOTING the speed and sea-keeping qualities in the design of small cruising yachts, originated in America before the First World War. However, the history of offshore racing in a broader and less purposeful form can be traced back into the nineteenth century. As early as 1833 Lord Belfast was racing off the British coast in his famous brig *Waterwitch*, when he defeated Mr Talbot's schooner *Galatea* over a 224-mile course, sailed from the Nab round the Eddystone lighthouse and back in rough conditions.

In 1866 three American schooners sailed across the Atlantic in one of the greatest yacht races of all time. The schooners were called *Henrietta, Fleetwing* and *Vesta* and the race took place in December, each owner having staked $30,000 on the result. The conditions for the event were drawn up during the brandy stage of a yachtsman's dinner at the New York Union Club, when George and Franklin Osgood wagered that their schooner *Fleetwing* would beat Pierre Lorillard Jnr's *Vesta* from Sandy Hook to Cowes, England. These three young blades were soon joined in their venture by James Gordon Bennett who paid his $30,000 to bring *Henrietta* into the contest. Bennett's greatest joy, apart from yachting, was to drive a coach and four at speed along the country roads of New Jersey at midnight, sitting stark naked on the box, cracking his whip and yelling ferociously; a pastime which nicely sums up the spirit of the first transatlantic yacht race.

The three schooners were similar in design, measuring between 105 ft. and 107 ft. in length. *Henrietta* and *Fleetwing* were both keelboats, *Vesta* had a centre-board. As may be imagined all three owners experienced some difficulty in raising a crew to race the Atlantic in mid-winter. The Osgoods were forced to sign on nine whaler captains in order to bring *Fleetwing*'s crew to its full strength. The arrangements were completed and at one o'clock in the afternoon on 11th December the three schooners pushed out past Sandy Hook for the open sea. James Gordon Bennett was the only owner to sail aboard his yacht.

For the next five days the schooners raced with hard reaching winds, battling through snow storms, sometimes maintaining a full spread of canvas, sometimes reefed, seldom at less than 10 knots. *Vesta* was the early leader, being overhauled on the fourth day by *Henrietta*. Of course, the yachts raced out of each other's sight and the skippers had no idea of their positions in the race until they reached Cowes.

In New York, the news of the race was spasmodic and unreliable. It was confined to reports from merchant ships which had sighted one or other of the competitors. On each sighting the city's gambling fraternity would enter a frenzy of renewed wagers.

By the evening of 18th December *Henrietta* had established a commanding lead, with *Vesta* 119 miles astern in second place and *Fleetwing* trailing a further 42 miles behind that. The south-west wind rose to gale force during the night and *Henrietta* hove-to for 8 hours. The same gale brought tragedy to *Fleetwing* when a huge sea swept into her cockpit and carried

Ocean racers in the Solent.

The schooners **Henrietta, Fleetwing** and **Vesta,** raced across the Atlantic in mid-winter 1866. One of the most dramatic ocean races of all time.

eight crew members overboard. Only two of them were recovered in the ensuing search which lasted for 5 hours.

However, while the two keelboats were hove-to during part of the night on 18th December, the centre-boarder *Vesta* kept going under a reefed staysail, a remarkable achievement for a yacht with no outside ballast. Her skipper ran her before the gale, NE by E, and although this took him diagonally across *Henrietta*'s wake, by dawn the gap between the two yachts had narrowed from 119 to 10 miles. By then the gale had abated sufficiently for *Vesta* to resume a more easterly course. The next day she went into the lead by a couple of miles. The race lay between these two yachts with *Fleetwing*, incapacitated and demoralized by her loss of crew, continuing to trail the field.

As the schooners closed on Bishop Rock off the Scilly Isles, the sum total of wagers laid on the result in New York exceeded one and a quarter million dollars. *Vesta* made her landfall at 6.55 p.m. on 24th December, just 50 minutes ahead of *Henrietta*. At this point it looked as though Pierre Lorillard would be taking the $90,000 winner's cheque. Unfortunately, his skipper let him down and spent the best part of the day losing *Vesta* in the English Channel and tangling with unreliable pilots. While he was fooling about in the fog *Henrietta* slipped through to victory, with a time for the voyage of 13 days, 22 hours and 46 minutes. It was 12.40 p.m. on Christmas Day and *Henrietta*'s crew could enjoy their turkey dinner at anchor. *Vesta*, the first boat into the Channel had to face the ignominy of finishing last, a day behind the winner and forty minutes after *Fleetwing* had berthed at Cowes.

James Gordon Bennett, matured by the race, returned to New York and became a more responsible citizen. He assumed control of the family newspaper, the *Herald*, and despatched Stanley to find Livingstone. He never lost his enthusiasm for yachting and in

1870 he raced across the Atlantic from east to west in his new 120 ft. schooner *Dauntless*, against Mr James Ashbury's schooner *Cambria*. which was on her way to challenge for the America's Cup. A monstrous Victorian silver tea service was the prize for this race and Ashbury won it with an hour and a half to spare over his opponent after 23 days of sailing. Bennett and *Dauntless* set off across the Atlantic again in 1887 but this time they were soundly thrashed by a new schooner called *Coronet*. Neither of these two Atlantic contests could match the atmosphere which pervaded that first great race of 1866, no other ocean race quite like it has ever been sailed.

In 1905 the German Kaiser attempted to revive some of the glamour which had attached to *Henrietta*'s victory in 1866, by presenting a solid gold trophy for a race across the Atlantic. Several majestic yachts lumbered up to the starting line in this dull event, including two auxiliary steam yachts with their propellers removed (*Sunbeam* and *Valhalla*).

The Kaiser's Cup was won easily by the great three-masted schooner *Atlantic* in the record time of 12 days, 4 hours 1 minute, with an average speed of 10·32 knots and a best day's run of 312 miles. Since she measured 185 ft. in length and carried more than 18,000 sq. ft. of working canvas, this remarkable vessel was able to keep with her during the race a depression which brought strong quartering winds to drive her along. *Atlantic*'s record is unlikely to be beaten because today's smaller yachts, however well designed, could not hold the required maximum speed potential. Apart from *Atlantic*'s splendid performance the 1905 race aroused little public enthusiasm, even the 'solid gold' cup turned out to be made of base metal, very thinly plated, on being melted down in 1914 to help the war effort.

The activities of Thomas Fleming Day, editor of the American magazine *Rudder*, were much more exciting than the Kaiser's Cup race and although they met with some suspicion at the time they bore great relevance to the future course of yacht racing. Day maintained that small boats were just as safe at sea as the large schooners and to prove it he organized a race in 1904 to be run from Brooklyn to Marblehead, a distance of 330 miles round Cape Cod. Six yachts started in the race, none of them measured more than 30 ft. on the waterline and all of them finished the course, Day coming last in his 19 ft. *Sea Bird*.

A number of American yachtsmen thought Day a lunatic for risking his neck in such a small boat so far out to sea, and what is more they said so in the newspapers. Day defended himself with impeccable style in the *Rudder*. The following excerpt from his article is one of the classics of yachting literature.

'Newspaper men ought to know better than to consult a lot of grey-headed, rum-soaked piazza scows,' he wrote. 'What do these miserable old hulks, who spend their days swigging booze on the front stoop of a clubhouse, know about the dangers of the deep? If they make a voyage from Larchmont to Cow Bay in a 10-knot breeze it is the event of their lives, an experience they never forget and never want to repeat.'

After this outburst Day ignored the 'miserable hulks' and soldiered on with his idea of ocean racing. His enterprises became more ambitious and more controversial as time wore on. In 1905 he organized a race from Brooklyn to Hampton Roads and in 1906 he ran the first Bermuda race. The announcement of the latter delighted the Cassandras who foretold a dozen ways to die aboard a small yacht in the grip of a Gulf Stream hurricane.

Day's first Bermuda race was not an unqualified success, although it was not wrecked by a hurricane and no lives were lost. Only three competitors turned up at the start, ranging from 40 ft. overall to 28 ft. Two of them finished the course, *Tamerlane* defeating *Gauntlett* and reaching Bermuda in 126 hours 9 minutes. (This time can be compared with *Bolero*'s record breaking run of 70 hours 11 minutes 4 seconds in the 1956 Bermuda race.)

In spite of the small field, modern ocean racing began with the 1906 Bermuda race. Later in the same year the first race across the Pacific was run from the West Coast, Los Angeles to Honolulu. It was won by the 80 ft. keel schooner *Lurline*. Between 1906 and 1910 the Bermuda race was held regularly, while the Honolulu race was sailed five times between 1906 and 1924. It is important to remember that few yachts took part in these early races, the field usually comprising five or six yachts handled by a hard core of enthusiasts. To the majority of yachtsmen, 'piazza scows' if you like, yachting meant a turn round the buoys. Nevertheless, during the years from 1906 to 1924 Day and his friends were building up the offshore fleet.

After the war the Bermuda race was revived in 1923 and run again in 1924, again with small entries. The significant event in the development of ocean racing at this time was the founding in 1922 of the Cruising Club of America. In 1923 members of the new club led by Herbert Stone, the editor of *Yachting*, unofficially organized the Bermuda race. Stone laid down the basic philosophy of ocean racing when he wrote that the purpose of the race was 'to encourage the designing, building and sailing of small, seaworthy yachts, to make popular cruising upon deep water, to develop in the amateur sailor a love of true seamanship and to give the opportunity to become proficient in the art of navigation. . . . In drawing the conditions of this race the Committee in charge has borne in mind that the race is primarily to furnish a test of boats of the new cruising type that designers have evolved in the last few years.'

The emphasis was on cruising rather than on racing but this had precisely the effect that Stone and his committee intended and marked the development of a new type of fast cruising yacht in the United States, the ocean racer.

All this activity in America could not pass unnoticed by British yachtsmen for long.

A recent development, which could shape the future of the sport, has been the organization of offshore racing between yachts without handicap. The **One Ton Cup**, evolved and administered by France, has produced a formula for reducing yachts of various sizes to a single rating. The first yachts built specifically for One Ton Cup competition appeared for the 1964 event, held off Copenhagen when the American yachts proved most successful. Dick Carter's **Tina** coming first with **Robin** in second place.

One Ton Cup competition is still in its early stages and it is a little difficult to anticipate its future progress. Perhaps the greatest danger which confronts the design of yachts to a single rating is the tendency to produce out and out racing machines and to sacrifice the cruising factor, essential in the design of ocean racers which compete under handicap.

(below) Captain John Illingworth's controversial **Maid of Malham** gave a much needed jolt to British ocean racer design before the war and pioneered the use of a masthead rig.

124

Messrs George and Franklin Osgood's schooner **Fleetwing.** Eight of her crew were lost at sea during the race across the Atlantic in 1866.

Weston Martyr, an English cruising enthusiast, raced in the 1923 and the 1924 Bermuda events and enjoyed them so much that on his return to England he set about the task of promoting the idea of a British ocean race, and a race round the Fastnet rock resulted from these efforts in 1925.

Only seven competitors, a distinctly shaggy bunch, started from Ryde in the Isle of Wight in the first Fastnet. The Havre pilot cutter *Jolie Brise* emerged the winner, completing the course in 6 days and just under 3 hours. The Ocean Racing Club was founded the following day with Sir Philip Hunloke as its first president and Herbert Stone elected American Representative on its Committee.

By 1926 the essential structure of the sport had been formed. The next 20 years leading up to the Second World War were years of consolidation. During this time the nature of the races themselves, the calibre of the yachtsman, the designers and the development of the ocean racer as a special kind of yacht, combined to build up the sport to a pitch which would survive the war to promote ocean racing as the growth sector within the entire field of yachting.

Each of the original classic ocean races has its own special character. The Bermuda covers 600 miles of a direct ocean course in weather which is reasonably predictable. The navigational difficulty in the race is to gauge the strength of the Gulf Stream's East-North-Easterly set. The Transpacific race, on the other hand, follows a much easier course for the navigator

James Gordon Bennett's **Dauntless** was beaten by the America's Cup challenger Cambria in their trans-Atlantic duel of 1870.

in weather which is almost always good and where there is never any fog. The feature of the Transpac (biennial from 1926) is its considerable distance of 2,300 miles, nearly four times as long as the Bermuda.

The Fastnet race is a 600 miler and is run under conditions which are probably more variable than in any other ocean race. The first part of the Fastnet gives more of an offshore than a true ocean course as it runs along the south coast of England. This means that navigators have to bear in mind both shores of the English Channel and the fierce tides and overfalls off some of the headlands. Combined with these navigational hazards are the untrustworthy weather, the likelihood of fog and the crowded shipping lanes. However, at no time during the Fastnet race is a yacht more than 100 miles from a harbour. The Fastnet has been run as a biennial event from 1929.

In addition to the ocean racing classics which were run regularly between the wars, major transatlantic races were held in 1928 (to Spain), 1931 (to England) and 1935 (to Norway). During this period the Cruising Club of America and the Royal Ocean Racing Club also encouraged a number of shorter offshore races. On the American Circuit came the 284 miles St Petersburg-Havana race in 1930 (now run round the Florida peninsula to Fort Lauderdale); to be followed in 1934 by the 184 mile Miami-Naussau race. A unique event in which some of the new ocean racing enthusiasts competed was the Chicago-Mackinac Island race,

which covered a distance of 333 miles on the great lakes and which had been first run as far back as 1898. In England the R.O.R.C. started to run the 251 mile Channel Race in 1928 and organized its first foreign-going race to Santander in 1929 (435 miles). By then ocean racing had become a serious sport, demanding efficient organization.

It was clear from the Kaiser's Cup race across the Atlantic in 1905 that time allowances would have to be made if boats of different dimensions were to compete on equal terms. The competitors in that event, which was run without handicap, varied between 87 ft. and 135 ft. on the waterline. Before 1905 handicapping had not proved necessary, for instance the schooners *Henrietta*, *Fleetwing* and *Vesta* had all been similar in size. Thomas Day had recognized the necessity for creating a scale of time allowances and had introduced a rudimentary scale, based on a yacht's length, in the early Bermuda races.

The British R.O.R.C. and the Cruising Club of America experimented with various rating rules. For a short time it looked as if the two governing bodies in the sport would agree when the Americans ran their 1928 Bermuda and 1930 Transatlantic races under British rules. However, for 1932 the Cruising Club of America produced its own rules which were entirely different in principle from those of the R.O.R.C. Ocean racing is still run

(left and right) Ocean racers in the Middle Sea Race, Malta, 1969.

(left) The 28ft cutter **Gauntlet**, one of the three entries for the first Bermuda Race in 1906, when she was beaten by **Tamarlane.**

(right) Lord Macklay's 38ft cutter **Mistress**.

under different rules in America to those which govern the sport in Great Britain. Paradoxically two sets of rules have proved beneficial. From an administrative point of view it has been easier to rate ocean racers under national rules than it would have been to rate them under international rules. From the yachtsman's point of view local rules have produced yachts ideally suited to local conditions while designers have learnt a great deal from seeing their boats compete on both sides of the Atlantic under both sets of rules.

So much for the structure of the sport, now for the yachts; great ocean racing yachts tend to fall naturally under two classifications, the great old lovables and the great trendsetters. The majority of the early yachts fell naturally into the old lovable league. Most of them were direct descendants of workboats. In the States designers like William Hand of New Bedford

(left and right) The great three-masted schooner **Atlantic** won the Kaiser's Cup in the record time of twelve days, four hours, one minute.

and John Alden of Boston based their first ocean racers on the lines of the New England fishing schooners. Alden, known as John O'Boston, followed Thomas Day as the great man of the Bermuda race. Between 1910 and 1954 he sailed thirteen Bermudas, winning the 1923, 1926 and 1932 races outright with *Malabar IV*, *Malabar VII* and *Malabar X* respectively.

Of the seven yachts to come to the starting line for England's first Fastnet race in 1925, only two had been designed specifically as yachts. The remainder had been converted from commercial use. Two of them were old Bristol Channel pilot cutters and two of them were Norwegian fishing ketches of the type designed by Colin Archer. The winner, *Jolie Brise*, had been built by M. Paumelle in 1913 as a Le Havre pilot boat and measured 48 ft. on the waterline. *Jolie Brise* had a great career in ocean racing under two of her owners, E. G. Martin and Robert Somerset, winning two more Fastnets (in 1929 and 1930), and coming first in her class in the R.O.R.C. Santander race of 1929.

The second Fastnet race in 1926 was won on corrected time by another traditional yacht, the cutter *Ilex*, owned by the Royal Engineers Yacht Club, which measured 40 ft. on the waterline with a beam of 10·4 ft. and had been built in 1899. *Ilex* was rigged as a yawl later and went on winning races up to the outbreak of war. She won the Santander race in 1930.

The 1926 Fastnet also saw the appearance of a British yacht built specifically to win the race. This first genuine British ocean racer was called *Hallowe'en* and was designed by William Fife for Colonel Baxendale. *Hallowe'en* was based on the lines of the inshore 15 Metre yachts, but more heavily constructed and modified to suit her for the rougher conditions of offshore

racing. With a 50 ft. waterline length *Hallowe'en*'s remarkable elapsed time for the Fastnet course in 1926 was 3 days 19 hours 5 minutes. With the appearance of *Hallowe'en* in England, yachtsmen had a foretaste of the direction in which the design of ocean racers would develop on both sides of the Atlantic during the thirties. In retrospect it seems extraordinary that British yachtsmen were so slow to experiment after her remarkable debut.

The first great trendsetting ocean racing yachts were all designed in America, and three of them in particular were responsible for changing the whole atmosphere and purpose behind the sport. They were *Nina*, *Stormy Weather* and *Dorade*.

The schooner *Nina* was designed by Starling Burgess in 1928 for Mr Paul Hammond and

(left and right) The 73ft overall ketch **Stormvogel** was built in 1961. She was designed by a consortium comprising Laurent Giles, E. G. Van de Stadt and Illingworth and Primrose for her South African owner Mr C. Bruynzeel. South Africa's greatest ocean racer finished first in the 1961 Fastnet and won the San Sebastian-Belle Ile race in 1962, coming first in Class I in the 1963 Skaw race.

built at great cost for the express purpose of winning the Transatlantic race to Spain, which she did. After this victory she came to England and won the 1928 Fastnet without much difficulty in the hands of Sherman Hoyt. British yachtsmen were outraged by her design, claiming that her mainmast had been stepped so far forward merely to cheat the rules, that her sawn-off counter and snubbed forward overhang were designed to the same purpose. Below deck, *Nina*'s lack of bulkheads and the fact that she had virtually an open cabin from the cockpit to the forepeak brought charges against her construction as being too light. However, as Sherman Hoyt pointed out, *Nina* had proved her seaworthiness by crossing the Atlantic and the Bay of Biscay, and with little time for a refit she had completed the Fastnet course—all without the slightest damage to her hull or rig. It seems that the real cause of the storm was *Nina*'s success and the fact that she had been designed and built regardless of cost, and sailed by experts with the sole purpose of winning. Such determination was considered unsporting by British yachtsmen, many of whom believed that their greatest military victory had been won on the playing fields of Eton.

Nina was eventually purchased by Mr de Coursey Fales and went on winning races under

352

(left and right) John Illingworth's **Myth of Malham** built in 1947, has proved to be the most successful British ocean racer since the war. Her most notable victories in a long list of racing successes include the Fastnets of 1947 and 1949. She was a member of the winning British team in the 1957 Admiral's Cup and was still a powerful contender in 1964, when she won her class in the Cowes-Dinard race.

a variety of modifications. In 1962 she delivered her last and perhaps her greatest shock to yachtsmen by winning the Bermuda race outright at the age of thirty-four. No longer a trendsetter in 1962, *Nina* must be one of the most original, most lovable and greatest yachts in the history of ocean racing.

Nina established the idea of building boats specifically to win ocean races but her design, which was rather eccentric, did not have a marked influence on the development of this new

Royal yawl **Bloodhound** leads Eric Tabarly's **Pen Duick III** at Cowes.

kind of yacht. The 52 ft. overall *Dorade*, designed by Olin Stephens in 1930, proved to be a real trendsetter in the design of ocean racers.

Olin Stephens was a young man in 1930 but he had already made a name for himself by designing some outstanding 6 Metre and 8 Metre yachts to the International Yacht Racing Union rule. *Dorade*'s lines were in many respects similar to those of an 8 Metre and markedly un-American. Like the British yacht *Hallowe'en* she was an offshore version of an inshore racing yacht. *Dorade* was a fairly light, deep, narrow boat with pronounced overhang. Stephens rigged her as a yawl to gain extra sail area (her mizen and staysail were not taxed by the rule). He also designed for her a double headsail rig with widely separated headstays and, for light weather, a big genoa set to her masthead.

Dorade's first outing in the 1930 Bermuda race was successful, although she finished third behind more traditional Alden designed schooners. By 1931, however, Olin Stephens and his younger brother Rod had their new yawl in peak tune and *Dorade* won the Transatlantic race to England by the staggering margin of 2 days. She followed up this victory by taking

A group of ocean racers taking part in the Britannia Cup during Cowes Week.

the 1931 Fastnet race. The Stephens brothers returned to a tickertape welcome in New York and a bookload of new orders for their design firm.

Dorade won her class in the 1932 Bermuda race and returned to England in 1933 to win the Fastnet for the second time running. In 1936, under new ownership, she won the Transpacific race to complete her superb record in the World's ocean racing classics. *Dorade* signalled the end of the popularity for the schooner rig in ocean racing and began the ascendancy of the yawl.

In 1935 Stephens designed a new yawl called *Stormy Weather* for Philip Le Boutillier. Larger and with more beam than *Dorade*, she had a waterline length of 39 ft. 8 in., a beam of 12 ft. 6 in., a draught of 7 ft. 10 in. and carried 1,300 sq. ft. of sail. Like the earlier Stephens boat she won the Transatlantic race (to Norway in 1935) and the following Fastnet.

Yachts designed by Olin Stephens had won both the Transatlantic races in 1931 and 1935, and three Fastnets in a row between 1930 and 1935. British yachtsmen were demoralized by the American domination of the ocean racing scene. A member of the R.O.R.C.

The launching of **Dorade**, designed by Olin Stephens, marked the beginning of a new era in ocean racing. She won the Transatlantic race and the Fastnet in 1931 and the Fastnet of 1933.

commented bitterly that the only way for the British to win a Fastnet race again was by annihilating Sherman Hoyt and the Stephens brothers with the starting cannons of the Royal Yacht Squadron battery. The enthusiasm for ocean racing continued to grow, however, and eighteen British yachts came to the start of the 1937 Fastnet. New ocean racers were commissioned and British designers were given more work to get their teeth into.

Charles Nicholson produced two famous ocean racers for Mr Issac Bell, a cutter called *Foxhound* which came fourth in the 1935 Fastnet behind *Stormy Weather* and a yawl, *Bloodhound*, which won the 1939 Fastnet (in the absence of American competition). 'Iky' Bell was an American and a nephew of James Gordon Bennett who spent most of his life in the British Isles. His *Bloodhound* incorporated the latest techniques of design, although not a great trendsetting yacht like *Dorade* she classifies for an old lovable label. Still racing today, until recently under the ownership of H.M. Queen Elizabeth, *Bloodhound* has notched up an impressive list of overall and class wins in most of the European offshore races since winning that 1939 Fastnet.

Captain John Illingworth's *Maid of Malham* was the pre-war British trendsetter. This 48 ft. overall cutter was designed by Laurent Giles in 1937 and had a most successful two seasons in offshore racing before the war. Her bow sections were lean and her keel cutaway, but the most singular thing about her was that she carried a masthead rig (the foresail was set from the top of the mast as opposed to from a point some way down it).

Of course *Maid of Malham* came in for a great deal of criticism, as all the best trendsetting ocean racers do. But as the war approached to put a stop to further activity, the British yachtsman Malden Heckstall-Smith answered her critics by saying: 'the best deep-sea racing craft which have yet been produced are far better cruisers than the large majority of so-called cruising yachts. They are faster—by any reasonable standard; they are better sea-boats;

Mr Paul Hammond's **Nina,** designed by Starling Burgess in 1928, won both the Transatlantic race and the Fastnet. Her design was extremely controversial at the time. One of the all-time greats, she won the Bermuda race in 1962 at the age of 34.

450

and they are far better and more substantially rigged and equipped. They are, in fact, deep-sea cruisers, and not just occasional cruisers.' His opinion was that ocean racing was achieving its primary objective in improving the design of cruising yachts.

Since the war Heckstall-Smith's judgment has been borne out. The great inshore racing yachts which sailed the regatta circuit of England and America in the twenties and thirties died with the war. Yet between 1950 and the present day yachting has proved to be one of the world's foremost growth sports. Today millions of small, family yachts combine cruising with club racing. Many of them are mass produced in glass fibre and all of them have developed directly from ocean racing, from yachts like *Dorade* and *Maid of Malham.*

To a certain extent the classic ocean races have taken over the prestige of the pre-war inshore circuit. Apart from the America's Cup it is into ocean racing that the modern yachtsman pours his big money. The 73 ft. yawl *Bolero* was built in 1949 for John N. Brown, Com-

(left) Mr H. T. Kaufman's **Mercedes III** was the highest points scorer in the victorious Australian Admiral's Cup team in 1967, finishing third overall in the Fastnet and winning the Britannia Cup.

(right) Olin Stephens' march through ocean racing was as relentless as General Patton's advance across Europe. After **Dorade** came **Stormy Weather,** which took the Transatlantic and the Fastnet races in 1935.

Major Bell's **Foxhound.**

modore of the New York Yacht Club, at a cost reputed to have been $300,000. Carelton Mitchell's $38\frac{1}{2}$ ft. *Finisterre* cost more than $75,000 in 1954. However the time allowance scale enables little men with smaller boats to compete on equal terms with these big spenders.

Ocean races, which before the war would have found the greatest difficulty in fielding over twenty yachts, now have their number of entrants limited. In 1956 the Bermuda had 89 entries, in 1958 the figure was 111 with 135 for the 1960 race. During the summer of 1967 no fewer than 14 offshore and ocean races were organized by the R.O.R.C. in Great Britain. In the R.O.R.C. points championship table for that season (divided into five classes), over

The cutter **Ilex** won the 1926 Fastnet.

400 yachts are listed. 139 yachts started in the Fastnet race and there were more than 100 starters in respectively the Round Gotland race (335 miles), Cowes to Dinard race (180 miles) and the Channel race (225 miles). The great ocean classics have continued to be run since the war in alternate years.

In 1947 John Illingworth commissioned a new 39 ft. cutter from Laurent Giles called *Myth of Malham*. Her design was highly controversial, producing a boat of light construction, with no sheer or bulwarks and with very short overhangs which skilfully evaded the depth and length measurements of the R.O.R.C. rating rule. A writer in the American journal

4519

(left) The yawl **Stella Polaris** racing in the Mediterranean.

(right) **Bloodhound,** a royal bottom.

Yachting described her as a 'dreadful-looking monstrosity', expressing the opinion that any designer or any rules that could produce such a boat ought to be hove overboard before the sport became contaminated. In fact *Myth of Malham* showed that a moderately light displacement yacht was not only a fast and seaworthy offshore racer, but could be built comparatively cheaply, an advantage which owners were quick to appreciate. She won the Fastnets of 1947 and 1949 outright and her class in 1957. She notched up class and outright wins in most of the R.O.R.C. offshore races and won the Fleming Day trophy for yachts under 40 ft. overall in the 1948 Bermuda race, finishing fourth in her class. A great trendsetter, *Myth of Malham* has proved the most successful British ocean racer since the war.

The trend towards smaller and cheaper light displacement yachts continued during the 1950s and a Transatlantic race between five British yachts which had competed in the 1950 Bermuda race was won by Adlard Coles on corrected time in the 23 ft. waterline *Cohoe*. With a sail area of 362 sq. ft. *Cohoe*'s time of 14 days, 7 hours 21 minutes for the race (under R.O.R.C. ratings) compares favourably with the 15 days, 2 hours 46 minutes taken by *Dorade* in 1931, carrying 1,150 sq. ft. of sail (and racing under C.C.A. rules). A similar event between British yachts in 1952 was won by the 24 ft. waterline *Samuel Pepys* skippered by Errol Bruce. Both these Transatlantic winners were substantially smaller than *Dorade* and both of them defeated larger yachts on corrected time.

Of the great post-war American ocean racers *Carina* and *Finisterre* are outstanding. *Carina* was a beamy, centre-board yawl setting 1,200 sq. ft. of sail on a waterline length of 36 ft. 3 in. She was designed for Richard S. Nye by Philip Rhodes in 1955 and proved to be a Fastnet specialist, winning outright in that year and in 1957, coming first in her class in 1959 and 1963. She also won the Transatlantic races to Sweden in 1955 and Spain in 1957 to dominate the European ocean racing scene. In contrast the Stephens-designed *Finisterre* dominated the American circuit, winning three Bermuda races in succession (1956, 1958 and 1960) for her owner Carleton Mitchell. Quite small by pre-war standards this $27\frac{1}{2}$ ft. waterline yawl was a centre-boarder like *Carina* and like *Carina* she was broad in the beam (11 ft. 3 in.). In her three victories she defeated more than three hundred competitors.

Perhaps the most significant aspect of the post war boom in ocean racing has been the development of the sport outside the traditional Anglo-American sphere of competition. Australia in particular has emerged not only as a challenger to American ocean racing supremacy but also as a challenger for the America's Cup.

The ascendancy of Australia as a yachting power began in 1945 when the Royal Yacht Club of Tasmania organized the first Australian classic ocean race from Sydney to Hobart, largely on the initiative of John Illingworth who was serving with the Royal Navy in Australia at the time. There were nine starters and the race was won by Illingworth in *Rani*.

The start of the Sydney–Hobart race—myriad spectator craft permitting—is at 11.00 on Boxing Day in Sydney Harbour and the finishing line runs across the Derwent River at Hobart. The course takes the competitors out through Sydney Heads, down the New South Wales and Victorian coasts, across the Bass Straight, round Tasman Light and up the Derwent River. The race is run under R.O.R.C. rules.

Conditions are wildly variable at this time of the year and although the start has been held more often than not in perfect summer weather, freak conditions can prevail even in the harbour itself. In 1957 the temperature was over 100 degrees and the surface was whipped to a frenzy by a hot westerly wind of 45 knots. The temperature can suddenly drop by 40 degrees with the almost instantaneous onset of the 'Southerly Buster' which reaches the height of its 100-knot fury in 'The Paddock', the hopefully placatory nickname for Bass Straight. 'The race begins again at Tasman Light' has become an accepted dictum because on several occasions the leaders have found themselves becalmed within a few miles of each other in the mouth of the Derwent River. Here the lightness of the breeze is further vitiated by confusing catspaws from the mountains, and by unpredictable tide-flows. In 1967 when only a few miles from the finish, Eric Tabarly in *Pen Duick III* watched his chances of the 'double' (first overall and on corrected time) ebb away as he had to kedge against the tide.

Sydney–Hobart has proved to be a successful ocean race and it has attracted many competitors from overseas, 1967 was a poor year for the Australians with Tabarly taking the Illingworth Trophy in *Pen Duick III* and the New Zealander *Rainbow II* winning on corrected time. But backing up the success story is the fantastic hold that the race has over the imagination of the non-participating public. Daily reporting of positions to the organizers by radio is obligatory. The local newspapers and radio stations, and more recently the television networks, headline progress reports and results of the race, displacing even current cricket Test matches. Now with the help of a Sydney-based computer, progress on corrected time is also broadcast daily. Even for the second race in 1946 the crowd watching the start from vantage points around the harbour was estimated at over a hundred thousand and it has grown annually. The number of spectators has increased correspondingly on, and sometimes in the water. The start has always been a pandemonium of spectator craft and more than one has been sunk by a competitor. A British entrant reported one year that a man paddling an ironing-board had capsized almost beneath her bow—and this in the shark-infested waters of Sydney Harbour!

Perhaps because of the incredible public interest more attention is paid in this race to the first across the line than in other offshore races. In the public eye the first to finish is demonstrably the winner, and so it is the winner of the Illingworth Trophy that the huge crowds in Hobart are waiting to see. When it is remembered that the race distance is 690 miles they have been treated to some very exciting finishes. They have also expended considerable applause on two yachts designed by Fife of Fairlie.

The 64 ft. cutter *Morna/Kurrewa* was built to a Fife design in Sydney in 1914 and later

Clear skies, clean decks, the yawl **Anahita** epitomises the beautifully functional in modern ocean racing.

modified with an Alan Payne designed cutter rig. She was the first to cross the line eight times. In 1960 she was involved in a tussle for line honours with another Fife boat—the 74 ft. schooner *Astor*. *Kurrewa* won, but the next year she did not compete and *Astor* had the first of her three victories. The fastest race was held in 1962 when S. A. Long's North American champion *Ondine*, a 58 ft. aluminium yawl, beat *Astor* by 62 seconds in a record time of 3 days, 3 hours, 47 minutes and 16 seconds. *Astor* won in 1963 and again in 1964.

Two other important dominators of the Sydney–Hobart race have been the naval architects, Alan Payne and the Halvorsen Brothers. In 1952 Payne won line honours with *Nocturne* a 35 ft. light displacement craft and in 1955 he designed *Solo* a steel cutter of 38 ft. 4 in. on the waterline. She was built by Mr Vic Meyer, her owner, in his own foundry and won on corrected time the 1956 race, which was sailed in conditions so tough that only half of the fleet of 28 starters finished. In the following two races *Solo* came second and first across the line. In 1959 she took line honours again in a race that was dominated by Alan Payne designs. She gave Payne another win on corrected time in the fast race of 1962.

The Halvorsen-designed *Freya*, which won in 1963 and completed a hat-trick in the next two years, was a brilliant demonstration of the power of accumulated experience. She was a new contender in 1963 and was a deliberate attempt to combine the best qualities of earlier Halvorsen yachts—*Peer Gynt, Solveig* and *Anitra V*. *Solveig* had won in 1954 and *Anitra V,* after winning in 1957, was beaten into second place in the succeeding two races by margins of only 8 and 20 minutes, to give the Halvorsens a record of twelve starts, two wins, five seconds and a third. *Freya,* in three races in varying conditions, proved herself

Two of the victorious Australian Admiral's Cup team in 1967. (left) Mr G. W. Ingate's **Caprice of Huon** and (right) Mr R. Crighton-Brown's **Balandra.**

H 536
H 536
124

an outstanding all-rounder and was selected to represent Australia in the 1965 Admiral's Cup.

The Admiral's Cup, presented to the R.O.R.C. in 1957 has played a crucial part in encouraging a more genuine international interest in ocean racing. Teams of yachts from any country can compete for the Cup. The rules stipulate that the teams must be of three, four or five yachts of not less than 30 ft. waterline. Each team competes in the Channel race, the Fastnet and two races run during Cowes Week, the Britannia Cup and the New York Yacht Club Trophy. The winners are the team to score the highest number of points in these races.

The first Admiral's Cup became a contest between Great Britain and America. The trophy was won by Britain, represented by *Uomie, Jocasta* and *Myth of Malham.* The British won again in 1959 with a Dutch team taking second place. The 1959 Fastnet had a record entry including yachts from Holland, France, Sweden, America, Belgium and Italy. It was won by the Swedish yawl *Anitra,* designed by Sparkmam and Stephens. The 1959 Round Gotland race, run in the Baltic by the Royal Swedish Yacht Club, had an entry of over fifty Scandinavian ocean racers. By then the R.O.R.C. rating rules were in use in eighteen countries and ocean racing was mushrooming world wide.

International competition has continued to expand during the sixties. Although the Americans won the 1961 Admiral's Cup (with *Cyana, Figaro* and *Windrose*) and the British won it in 1963 and 1964, the Australians arrived in 1967 to make the first successful challenge to Anglo-American yachting supremacy. The Australian victory in the 1967 Admiral's Cup series with *Caprice of Huon, Mercedes II* and *Balandra* provides a seamark in yachting history. In 1961 the first great South African ocean racer *Stormvogel* was launched, while the French single-handed yachtsman Eric Tabarly has continued to experiment with his *Pen Duicks,* winning the 1967 Fastnet with *Pen Duick III.*

Ocean racing has advanced a long way from Thomas Fleming Day's first Bermuda race in 1905, and the impetus to international competition promoted since the war augurs a healthy future for the sport.

(left) A most important aspect of design development within ocean racing has been the proliferation of small, seaworthy and relatively cheap yachts that can be used by the family for both racing and cruising.

(right) Eric Tabarly's wishbone schooner **Pen Duick II** rounding Fastnet rock.

86
24

Great Dinghies, Small Yachts

NOWADAYS THERE IS NO INFLEXIBLE MINIMUM SIZE FOR A GREAT YACHT CLASS; AND THE greatness of some of the contemporary classes is due to the size of their fleet, or the standard either of helmsmanship or design, or to some more elusive factor, such as their effect on the overall development of yachting.

The end of the First World War saw the rise of the smaller keelboat and dinghy classes, boats sailed not by a professional skipper but by their owner, and crewed more frequently by his friends than by paid hands. The Second World War brought an end to many great yachts as well as a temporary halt to these new developments, perpetuated in the early post war years by a shortage of boatbuilding materials. However, the war was responsible for the development of new materials such as resin-bonded plywood and aircraft alloys, which joined the traditional Honduras mahogany and Sitka spruce once the supply lines opened up again. The motor car and the home do-it-yourself craze played their part in a new popularity for dinghy sailing. The man who learned that he could put up a shelf found that he could also build his own boat. His car carried it to new centres on the coast and a post war boom in the sport began. This meteoric rise in numbers of do-it-yourself boats has, in turn, prompted an impressive increase in keelboats (especially of small cruising yachts).

The trend to great classes of small boats has been accelerated by the decline of the larger ones. As 12 Metres (America's Cup racing apart), 8 Metres and 6 Metres became obsolete, so 5·5 Metres, Dragons and the host of National and local one-design classes grew stronger.

Although small boat sailing did not achieve any great stature within the sport of yachting until after the Second World War, it was popular in certain areas as early as 1870. Racing in 14 ft. dinghies began in England in the nineteenth century when relatively lightweight boats were taking the place of heavily ballasted yacht tenders of some 18 ft., in which small boat competition had been conducted hitherto. Of the various regional dinghies, the West of England Conference dinghy and the Norfolk dinghy were the most significant. The Conference dinghy was the older of the two, first recorded at Teignmouth in 1889. The Norfolk dinghies were different in concept, evolved for inland sailing and built to the Yare and Bure Sailing Club rules. In 1911 Morgan Giles, a West Country boat builder, wagered £50 that his Conference dinghy, *Firefly*, would beat Norfolk's best, which it did by winning four out of the five races in the match. After the First World War a National 14 ft. class was formed, developed from the Conference dinghy, and it became so popular that it was awarded International status in 1927. Between 1928 and 1939 Uffa Fox dominated the class, sailing his *Avenger* to 52 wins out of 57 starts and cruising her on a return voyage across the Channel to Le Havre. In 1938 Peter Scott, now chairman of the International Yacht Racing Union, won the class's premier event, the Prince of Wales Cup. In the same year and in conjunction with John Winter, he devised a trapeze harness, but its use was banned on the International 14 which was built on a narrow beam in those days, although the modern hull is broader and the use of a trapeze harness in the class is now legal.

The post-war boom in yachting has centred round massive growth in dinghy and small cruiser classes.

The development of new materials has permitted great scope to designers and builders

The **Snipe** is the most popular dinghy class in the world with over 15,000 sail numbers registered.

of the International 14 ft. dinghy, so that glass-fibre, round-bilge boats now compete with others of hard-chine construction, built from plywood. Its place in any list of important yachts is not merely a matter of the current class's speed but of its undoubted influence on the sport of yachting. The International 14 ft. class provides the foundation of small boat sailing in Great Britain and the basis on which many other classes have been built. Its international status has encouraged large fleets to appear outside Great Britain, particularly in America, Canada and New Zealand, and Stewart Morris, who has won the Prince of Wales Cup on no less than twelve occasions between 1932 and 1965, must be considered as one of the greatest dinghy helmsmen in the world.

The foundation of small boat sailing in America is not so easy to locate and one cannot select a single class to hold a position as fundamental as that held in Great Britain by the International 14 ft. dinghy. Racing is recorded in New York waters as early as 1840 with a variety of small craft measuring between 20 to 30 ft. long and known as sandbaggers because of the methods employed to ballast their narrow centre-board hulls. The New York Canoe Club was established in 1871 and it was shortly after this date that the idea of international competition in small boat racing evolved, when an annual canoe race between Great Britain and America was suggested. In 1895 it was a member of the Canoe Club who instigated the presentation of the Seawanhaka International Trophy. The racing of canoes and scows was pioneered in America and the modern International 10 sq. m. canoe, measuring between 16 and 17 ft. and carrying a single crew on a sliding seat, can claim to be the fastest single hulled centre-board in the world.

The growth of small boat sailing in America to its current popularity is based on the development of the Star class in 1911 and was accelerated by the introduction of the Snipe class in 1931. The Snipe is the smaller of the two boats. It measures $15\frac{1}{2}$ ft. long and whether one regards it as a dinghy or as a yacht there can be no doubt as to the greatness of its class and its key position in yachting history. This position is maintained by the ever increasing size of the class fleet. The Snipe is a sluggish performer by modern standards but as the most popular one-design class, with around 15,000 members registered, it offers the sailor the best chance of obtaining top competition not only in America but all over the world. Originally evolved under sponsorship from the American Yachting magazine *Rudder* the Snipe was designed by William F. Crosbie and first appeared off Florida in 1931. The class rules specified that the hull should weigh not less than 440 lbs which provided a heavy load to be driven by a relatively small sail area (116 sq. ft.). Nevertheless, it was intended that the Snipe

The **Soling** was designed as a possible Olympic successor to the **Dragon**.

should be home built for under $100 and it was this specific object of its design which brought it such outstanding popularity. The Snipe class dinghy, together with the International 14, can be regarded as responsible for bringing the sport of yachting within the reach of a new public, and its success during the thirties laid the foundations for the post war boom in small boat sailing which has formed such a significant part of the contemporary yachting scene.

However, if the Snipe pioneered the way for sailing on a small budget at one end of the scale, without pressing for speed as a design priority, rising costs were responsible for new developments at the other end of the scale, where speed was regarded as essential.

Charles Nicholson, the yacht designer, and Major Malden Hackstall-Smith were the two famous British names behind the development of the 5·5 Metre, which they intended as a replacement for the 6 Metre class, the costs of which were becoming prohibitive. The Nicholson/Heckstall-Smith formula was evolved in 1912, used for the 1920 International 18 ft. class, revived in 1949, and was adopted by the International Yacht Racing Union in

America's Cup apart, the **5.5 metre** survives to reflect the pre-war concept of the big keelboats racing inshore round the buoys.

1950. It was designed to produce a boat in between the very light square metre boats developed in Scandinavia and the very heavy boats encouraged by the 12 Metre, 8 Metre and 6 Metre International Rules. It was based on the formula for A-class model yachts for which Nicholson and Heckstall-Smith were enthusiasts. In 1952 the 5·5 Metre class was accepted for the Olympic Games, which by that stage provided the focal point for the design of out-and-out inshore racing boats.

The 5·5 Metre was, until recently, the largest yacht sailed in the Olympics and although its Olympic place has now been taken by the Soling, it is still the development keelboat *par excellence*. Its formula effectively defines the broad dimensions of the class and ensures fair racing, while at the same time allowing designers freedom to turn their ideas and experience into faster and faster yachts. *Deb*, the 1949 prototype 5·5 Metre, would have next to no chance against today's class but 1969 designs proved little superior to those of 1966 and 1967, showing that the development curve is levelling. This enables an owner to commission a new boat with the possibility that it will remain competitive for several years.

The two-man keelboat **Tempest** was designed by Ian Proctor.

Thus pockets are not emptied too rapidly while the allure of design development remains.

1956 was the heyday of the British 5·5 Metre fleet with Lt.-Col. 'Stug' Perry winning an Olympic silver medal in the Arthur Robb designed *Vision*. The current 5·5 Metre, costing in the region of £4,000, is no economy model and the U.K. fleet has dwindled effectively to the solitary *Yeoman XV*, sailed by Robin Aisher, Paul Anderson and Adrian Jardine. Second in the 1967 World Championships and bronze medallist at Acapulco, Aisher has made a brave bid to top the class but British 5·5 Metre design has declined. Today the top designers are Arne Ohlsson of Sweden and the American, Britton Chance. Of the two Chance is the most opportunist, producing designs more *avant-garde* than those introduced in any other class.

The 5·5 Metre is not everyman's yacht. As a keelboat it provides a ride as fast and furious as any dinghy. The 5·5 Metre pack downwind, presents one of yachting's most cliff-hanging spectacles. Short keels to reduce hull friction are combined with big spinnakers to hold fat chunks of wind. With a fresh breeze on the beam the combination is lethal. The gaily coloured spinnakers burst full as soon as the fleet rounds its weather mark. Riding a bow wave like a

Lady Helmsman successfully defended three Little America's Cup competitions for Britain.

Cowes-Torquay powerboat, first one boat and then another takes the lead. The spinnaker is fighting against the keel to lay the boat on to its beam ends. As the first squall strikes, boat after boat is flattened before it. Spinnakers distort as the boats round up into the breeze, then suddenly empty their charge of air with a giant lunge and a crack of sheets like gunfire. It takes a courageous crew to hold their boat on its feet. One boat at the 1966 World Championships, held in Copenhagen, was laid so flat by its spinnaker that it filled and sank. One of the three-man crew had his foot held by a rope and went to Davy Jones's locker with the boat. Fortunately the manned submersible hit the bottom with a jolt sufficient to release the crew, who then surfaced in good condition.

The largest Olympic yacht, now that the 5·5 Metre has been excluded from the competition, is the Dragon. Johan Anker, the famous Norwegian designer, drew the lines for this class in 1929, conforming to the old 20 sq. m. rules, and submitted them for a competition organized by the Royal Yacht Club of Gothenburg, Sweden, who were seeking the ideal racing keelboat which would also provide cruising accommodation for two. Johan Anker won this competition and the Dragon became established throughout Scandinavia and in Germany. *Anita,* owned by Jimmy Howden-Hume and Bill Paisley, was the first boat to arrive in Britain and the first British fleet was established on the Clyde when the Clyde Yacht Club's Conference adopted the class in 1935. By 1939 fleets were established around the U.K. coast.

The Clyde Yacht Club's Conference donated a Gold Cup in 1937 for annual racing in the Dragon class, with an unrestricted entry. The event was to take place, by rotation, in Scotland, Norway, Sweden, Denmark and Germany. In addition a European Championship Trophy was presented after the war, to be held annually with entry restricted to three boats per country, the venue to be in Europe. However, the Gold Cup continued to be the major trophy in the class until, in spite of increasing interest in North America, its ruling committee refused to open up the competition and the introduction of a world trophy became essential. The new biannual World Championship and the European Championship titles have now become pre-eminent.

Unlike the 5·5 Metre, the Dragon is a one-design boat which gives latitude for invention solely in details of gear and in the tolerances on key measurements allowed to the builder. Even this limited freedom provides adequate scope for ingenuity, shown by the considerable variation from boat to boat. Scandinavian builders and sailors dominated the fleet for years,

although a British helmsman, Martin Parry, won the European Championship in 1963 and Simon Tait, sailing *Blue Haze*, retained the trophy for Britain in 1965. Subsequently the Americans, whose interest was aroused by the class's Olympic status have stepped in with new ideas for spars, gear, sail-handling and functionally built boats. Buddy Friedrichs from New Orleans took the World Championship title in 1967 and the 1968 gold medal at Acapulco, sailing *Williwaw*.

The Dragon measures 29 ft. overall and costs two-thirds the price of a new 5·5 Metre. It is still an expensive boat now that its cruising function has been entirely displaced by the need for lightness and speed, the hulls having become empty shells. Magnificently constructed of edge-glued mahogany planks, the cost lies in the hand craftsmanship with which the hulls are assembled strip by strip and in the refinement of gear. A magnificent boat in a breeze, the Dragon is much more easily handled than the 5·5 Metre and following the adoption in 1945 of a new rig, carried a small spinnaker and an overlapping genoa jib. The present size of this class numbers 1,500 boats.

These are early days to judge the Dragon's rival, the Soling. It is surprising, however, that the quite different 5·5 Metre class should have been dropped from the Olympics in order to make room for the Soling, which was conceived as an eventual Olympic successor to the Dragon. The International Yacht Racing Union ran trials in 1966 to select a new three-man keelboat for International racing. The Soling, designed by the Norwegian Jan Herman Linge, proved astonishingly fast against bigger rivals in both these trials and in a second trial series run in 1967. Selected in 1967, the Soling class is already on the move world-wide.

Faster and cheaper (at £1,500) than the Dragon, the Soling's progress is inevitable now

The 5.5 pack downwind.

(left and overleaf) Between the wars inshore keelboat racing was at the core of the sport; after the second war it lost this key position to ocean racing and easily attainable, mass-production dinghies. The **Dragon** class has survived to provide the largest Olympic keelboat class.

(right) The **C class catamaran** is the fastest sailboat in the world.

C
K 16

D
K396
D

that the International Olympic Commission has voted the class into the Olympics. It is difficult to see the Dragon class holding its place alongside the Soling for long but with boats sailing all over the world, ranging from Japan to Finland, Brazil and Argentina it is deeply entrenched. A fleet worth some £3,000,000 cannot be replaced overnight.

The Star is the third Olympic keelboat class, with a keel formed by an iron bulb slung on a steel fin. The Star, together with the International Snipe, has been directly responsible for promoting small boat sailing in America. Originated by George A. Corry of Long Island the Star was designed in 1911 by Francis Sweisguth of the William Gardner Marine Architect Company. The 1911 Star was a monstrously heavy craft with a gaff rig, thick planks, a semi-flat bottom and chines but it cost only $600. Ike Smith of Port Washington L.I. built the first 22 boats as a 'poor man's one design yacht'; but, unlike the Snipe, the Star was designed essentially as a racing machine. It measured 22 ft. 7½ in. long against the Snipe's 15 ft. 6 in. and was correspondingly more expensive, with a heavy construction which was unsuitable for home building. Like the Snipe, the Star class has lasted well with sail numbers still increasing after 50 years in service. Today it is an anachronism amongst modern sailboats but even without taking into consideration its important position as a pioneer it can be judged as the greatest small keelboat of the age on character alone, attracting more of the world's top sailors for the Olympics than any other class.

Like its Olympic companions the Star is no longer cheap, but the contemporary boat is a joy to look at, with a finish on which even a water spider could not find a foothold and a razor sharp performance to windward in smooth water to exhilarate the most demanding expert. Having been designed with Long Island calms in mind the Star is over-canvassed

The Flying Dutchman **Superdocious** won an Olympic gold medal at Acapulco for British yachtsmen Rodney Pattisson and David Hunt.

but the German Walter Von Hutschler (nicknamed Pimm and sailing a boat called *Pimm*), showed how to control the vast sail area with a flexible mast, thus making use of the tremendous progress in bending aluminium spars (and incidentally kicking straps), one of the features of yacht racing today.

Ian Proctor leads the development in bending spars with his Ian Proctor metal masts. He has also designed the Tempest two-man keelboat, which was selected at the I.Y.R.U. trials at Medemblik, Holland, where it proved vastly superior to any other entry.

The Tempest is a lightweight, glass-fibre, 22-footer which carries 250 sq. ft. of sail and is balanced with a fin and bulb keel, retractable for transport, and by the weight of the crew suspended on a trapeze. In all but light winds the Tempest has proved conclusively that it is superior to the Star, with a fleet expanding at the rate of some 100 boats per annum. Although strong fleets are forming in the U.K., where its performance in a breeze and a seaway makes it far more suitable than the Star, it has yet to get its veteran rival into a deathlock. This rivalry is intense, so similar are the two boats from the crew's point of view, and although the Tempest was nominated Olympic successor to the Star, the latter has held its place for 1972. In the Star both helmsman and crew straddle the weather rail—which gives them a close-up view of, and an action-packed feeling towards, each and every wave under which they are about to be driven. In the Tempest the helmsman hangs out in a back-stretching, parallel-to-the-water situation, while the crew stands horizontally with his feet on the side of the boat, slung in mountaineering fashion by a trapeze wire attached to his body belt from a point high up the mast. You pay your money (about $3,000 or £1,500 for a Star and £950 for a Tempest) and take your choice of two fast, wet and superlatively thoroughbred rides.

One other Olympic class has achieved greatness in a comparatively short time. The Flying Dutchman measures 19 ft. 10 in. and has a centre-board. U. Van Essen from Holland designed it in 1957 in the European tradition of big heavily canvassed, lake-type scows, but with its trapeze and windward power it has proved to be a fine seaboat. The Flying Dutchman won the I.Y.R.U. two-man centre-board trials and was selected for the 1960 Olympics. Numbering some 4,000 boats, the class has become one of the most international in existence. So fast are the Flying Dutchman downwind under spinnakers, and so demanding are they of crews as far as co-ordination, technique and physical fitness are concerned, that the Flying Dutchman sailor, no matter how badly he sails, commands a measure of respect.

The British Flying Dutchman fleet is small, containing only some 50 boats, but it provides the best competition in the world and leads in the development of new handling and tuning techniques. Rodney Pattisson and Iain Macdonald-Smith (currently Olympic gold medallists), John Oakeley and David Hunt (current World Champions), Keith Musto and Tony Morgan (ex-world champions and Olympic silver medallists) are crews of great ability, application and sportsmanship. To watch them compete is to see sailboats being driven as hard as a Grand Prix car, although the tactics which they employ are closer to those involved in a game of chess.

One other new kind of boat cannot be classified as a dinghy or a keelboat, but nevertheless promises to play a major role in the future development of the yacht. The development of the multihulled yacht for ocean racing, single-handed sailing and for cruising rests largely on the early progress of the Catamaran for inshore racing.

Multihull boats have been in use in Malaya and the Polynesian Islands for centuries and an early European twin-hulled boat was designed by Sir William Petty, the English boat-builder, in the reign of Charles II. In the late nineteenth century, the great American designer, Nat Herreshoff, startled the New York Yacht Club by racing a catamaran of his own design. However, the club disallowed this advanced machine from racing under club rules and it was not until the late 1950s that multihull boats made any significant impact on a conventionally monohulled yachting world. Roland and Francis Prout, British Olympic canoeists, together with Ken Pearce pioneered the design of small racing catamarans, and in America the appearance of these catamarans at a special one-of-a-kind regatta, held in Florida in 1959 by the magazine *Yachting*, proved them faster than any of the monohull boats with which they competed, though they came second to the American *Tigercat*.

In 1959 John Fisk, Commodore of the Chapman Sands Sailing Club in Essex, challenged

(left) Look no feet! **Star** showing them a fine pair of heels.

(right) **Dragon** flying.

D
K320
K320

Star class racing started in 1911. Originally designed as a poor man's one-design yacht a star costs about $3,000 today.

the Americans to a catamaran race. The Sea Cliff Yacht Club accepted the challenge but no contest materialized until 1961, when the Americans presented the International Catamaran Challenge Trophy (better known as the Little America's Cup), specifying that the match should take place over seven races, the winner of the match being the first boat to win four of them. Great Britain won the first series when John Fisk and Rod Macalpine-Downie sailing *Hellcat II* beat John Beery and John Hickock in *Wildcat*. From these catamarans were drawn the rules of the International 'C' class. Recognized by the I.Y.R.U. International 'C' class catamarans must be manned by two persons, have a maximum extreme beam of 14 ft. and may not measure more than 25 ft. in length. Capable of speeds in excess of 30 knots, they must be considered as the fastest and most exciting boats in the world.

Great Britain successfully defended the Little America's Cup on seven occasions, four American and three Australian challenges. A close series was sailed in 1965 when *Emma Hamilton* defeated the Australian challenger, *Quest II*, by four races to three. Rod Macalpine-Downie has proved to be the most successful designer and he is already concerned with the development of larger catamarans for ocean racing. Of the boats, *Lady Helmsman* has three defences of the Little America's Cup to her credit. Her unique wing mast, evolved by Clarence

International 14 class provides the foundation of small boat sailing in Great Britain.

Farrar, developed 30 h.p. Usually sailed by Reg White and John Osborn, *Lady Helmsman* ruled the catamaran seas for three years and has earned her place in yachting history.

In 1969 Britain lost the Little America's Cup, which it had held since the inception of the competition in 1961, to Denmark. The Danish boat *Opus III,* sailed by Gert Fredericksen and Leif Wagner Smitt, proved the faster design. At one time 3–1 down in the series, the Danes won the last three races to take the trophy.

The current direction of yachting towards smaller and smaller classes of boat, both in competitive and cruising circles, has come about gradually. On the one hand there are great dinghies, such as the International 14, the Snipe and the Flying Dutchman, and on the other hand there are the small yachts, such as the 5·5 Metre and the Dragon. The design of these great dinghies constituted a breakaway from the established concept of yachting, while the small yachts have maintained the original concept in extenuating circumstances. The 5·5 Metre was developed because the 6 Metre was becoming too expensive and the design of the Dragon conformed to the old 20 sq. m. rules. Now the design wheel has turned full circle and the development of multihull craft, on a small boat scale, promises to change much of the designer's thinking behind larger offshore racing and cruising yachts.

1802

The Cruising Yacht

VOYAGES ARE REMEMBERED FOR INCIDENT RATHER THAN COMPETENCE. ANYONE WHO MAKES a 30-mile cruise up the coast, devoid of dismastings, men overboard, or even of split oilskins, will be hard put to have an account of his adventures published. Let him run aground, encounter a recalcitrant tramp steamer or become entangled in some Tunny nets, however, then the first sparks of interest can be kindled in a thousand or so yachtsmen-occupied armchairs.

Joshua Slocum, about to meet the Fuegian Indians, stimulates the imagination with a wealth of anecdote. The bag of tin-tacks he received from a knowing sea captain at Punta Arenas is widely recalled, as is the advice that 'you must use them with discretion, that is to say, don't step on them yourself'.

William Hickey, cruising in the 1760s, found the accommodation aboard a 50-ton cutter 'capital' and went on to commend 'her spacious cabin aft . . . with sash windows astern'. Nice for Mr Hickey, but scarcely the stuff of sensation. Similarly Mr William Walker, who rounded the Horn in 1861 in the 72-ton schooner *Chance* (a yacht described as 'small' by Lord Dunraven) is not well remembered. This despite making a passage from Cowes to Sydney, westabout, in 141 days, and in mixed weather. A meritorious voyage indeed, but one inviting that damning comment of the school report: worthy but dull. How unfair!

The sensational voyages have contributed considerably to the development of the cruising yacht, for the 'development', in fact, has largely been a process of emancipation, a gradual realization that truly small craft, competently handled, can be quite at home in the open ocean.

An early emancipator, Knight, sailed the 28-ton *Falcon* to South America in 1880. Even earlier, R. T. McMullen had described his coastal voyages in the three-tonner *Leo*, in the 1850s. Although his passages were comparatively modest by the standards of Slocum or of the Atlantic-crossing 26-footer *Red White and Blue* (1866), he makes the point that coastal waters can be as tricky as any and that the proximity of land, in foul weather, can be as great a cause of disaster as the freak waves and mountainous seas still beloved of the popular press.

Slocum himself was an emancipator *par excellence*. His spirited account of the voyage of the *Liberdade*, in 1888, should not be eclipsed by his better-known *Sailing Alone Around the World*. In a sense the *Liberdade*'s passage from Rio to Washington D.C. was not a cruise in the conventional sense, for the Slocum family—wife, eighteen-year-old Victor and the other, and much younger, son Garfield—had all been stranded when the Captain's barque *Aquidneck* was wrecked and became a total loss. Slocum contemplating the *Liberdade*, an unfinished 35 ft. canoe with a beam of only 7 ft. 6 in., exclaimed 'Let's sail home in her and be a real shipwrecked crew'—and did that very thing.

Cruising under sail has been aided in recent years by racing practice, while voyages like that of Patrick Ellam and Colin Mudie in the 19 ft. 8 in. *Sopranino* in 1951–2, presaged the Armada of truly tiny craft crossing the Atlantic today and of which the crews can feel that they are indeed following a well worn track.

Christina, a handsome cruiser.

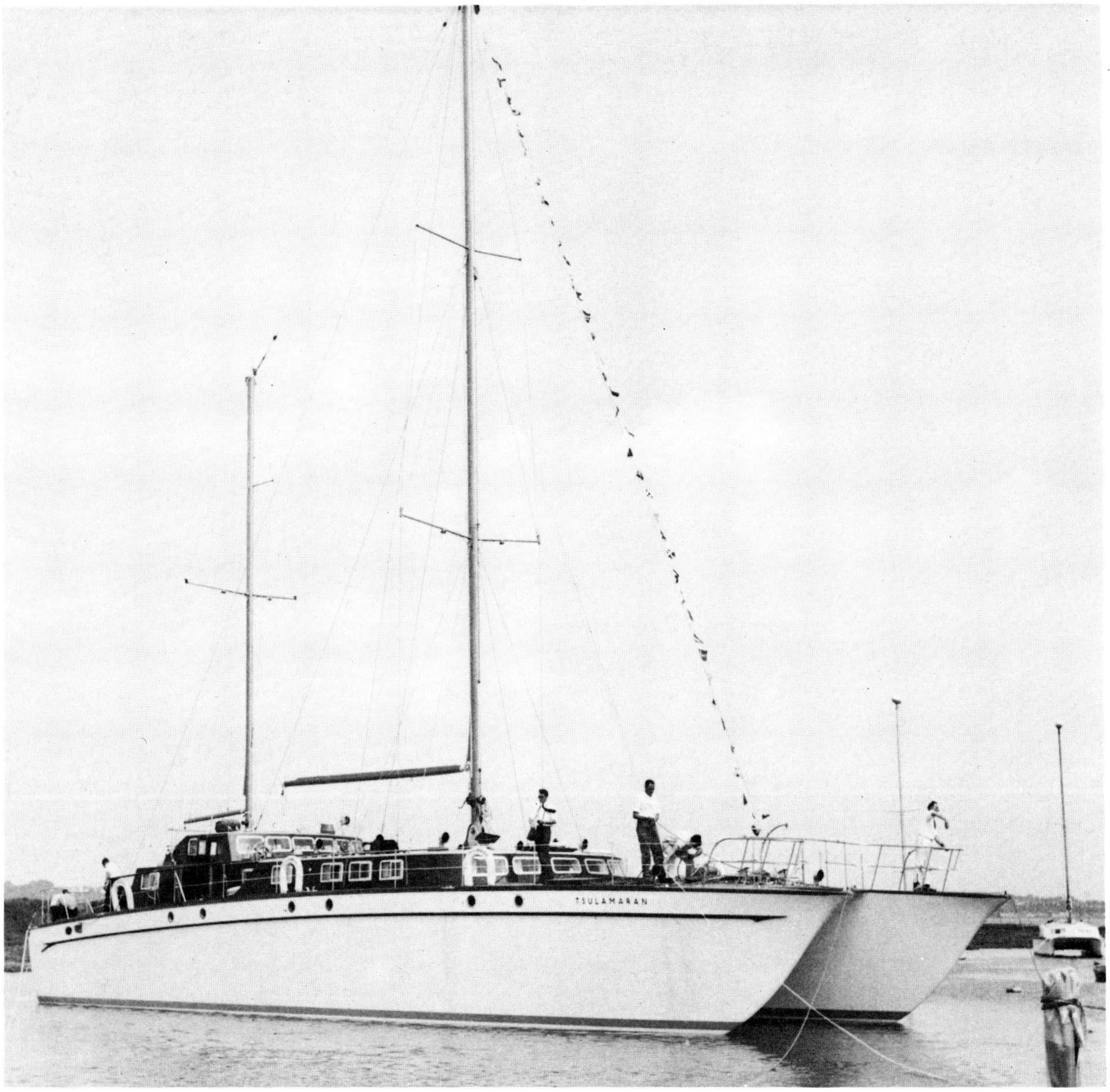

The 78ft **Tsulamaran.** Multi-hull yachts hold significant advantages for cruising in accommodation and speed. They must have a bright future, although as yet there is some question about their behaviour in bad weather.

Eric and Susan Hiscock, in recording their experiences in successive world-girdling *Wanderers* have written chapter and verse for potential followers. John Illingworth and Erroll Bruce, in their respective books *Offshore* (really an ocean racing manual) and *Deep Sea Sailing* have contributed invaluable text books on technique which enable the modern crop of small craft to survive and make good at sea. Today Transatlantic races, a Round the World event and tougher and tougher courses for racing powerboats help refine yacht design for sea-going. Men like Adlard Coles (also an expert and highly successful ocean racer) have liberated us from the ultra-cautious pilot books of earlier eras. Coles, who has himself ventured into the most hazard-strewn coastal waters, has recorded his findings in the most practical manner; his *Brittany Harbours and Anchorages*, for instance, has seen many a modern yachtsman to a mooring safely. Previous volumes on pilotage, big ship orientated, wary of the land, and stuffed with glum warnings against shoal, fever, and even cannibalism, have tended to discourage inquisitiveness along convoluted coastlines. Coles maintains a healthy balance of adventurousness and good seamanship, recognizes the hazards, where present, and has taken the trouble to discover in what conditions safe entry into such an unlikely haven as Molene, near Ushant, is possible—by trying it himself.

Thus we can explore what might be termed the psychological background to cruising. To cover its history more straightforwardly:

The earliest evidence of a cruising yacht is provided by a model in an Egyptian tomb, revealing the presence on the Nile in 1500 B.C. of at least one 100-ft. vessel, with a cabin, used for pleasure purposes. 'Modern' yachting developed on the rivers and lakes of Holland,

The successful American ocean racer, **Figaro.**

The design techniques evolved in ocean racing are incorporated in modern cruising yachts to the extent that it has become difficult to distinguish between cruising yachts and ocean racers as such.

where Charles II of England, a keen yachtsman, sailed whilst in exile. The Stuart yachts, in reality small ships, are well known, although sailing for pleasure in small workboats has obviously endured for much longer; Charles II himself derived his interest from boyhood experiences in a pinnace between the Channel Isles.

In the nineteenth century, we find ocean voyages being made for pleasure, rather than for trade or warfare. In *Letters from High Latitudes* Lord Dufferin recorded his visit to Iceland in the schooner *Foam*, while in 1864 the 150-ton schooner *Themis* rounded the world via the Horn, Vancouver and the China Seas. Nor were all the voyages in large craft. In 1864 Mr Sydney Bert and crew in the 25-ton cutter *Vivid* sailed 16,000 miles to Sydney in 130 days. The *Vivid,* incidentally, started life as the *Scourge* and was built primarily for racing in Dublin Bay. Other notable passages of the time were those of Knight, already mentioned; his crew, for

Golden Cockerel, one of the first cruising catamarans produced in Britain.

Major H. W. Tilman's famous old cutter **Mischief** in Arctic waters.

the record, consisted of 'three amateurs and one paid hand to do the cooking and cleaning up'. The 8-ton *Pet* cruised extensively in the Baltic, the *Alerte* visited Brazil in (unrequited) lust for treasure, while a contemporary account of the 500-mile passage of the 15-ton *Sonata* from Brightlingsea to Inverness is representative of the large numbers of such cruises made in 1882.

Although Lord Dunraven, writing in 1900, claims a close affinity between sailing cruisers and racers of the period, the workboat ancestry of many of the craft listed is apparent. In fact, in the next breath Dunraven badly weakened his argument by stating that the only variation in structure between the ideal racer and the ideal cruiser is that the former would probably be given more beam than is desirable for the latter. Racing vessels generally sail in smooth, or comparatively smooth, water, where initial natural stability derived from beam is advantageous . . . 'The enormous stability imparted to racers by heavy lead keels at great depth tells against them in a sea way; it causes their movements to be very rapid and violent; they plunge heavily, are very hard upon their gear, and particularly disagreeable to most human stomachs'.

Little was known about ballasting, witness the tragic capsize of the American schooner *Mohawk* in 1876, whilst lying at anchor with all sail set, inside Staten Island. The *Mohawk*, built as a racer but used for cruising, was knocked over by a sudden squall and capsized, drowning the owner, Mr Garner, his wife and four guests. At the time the *Mohawk* was, at 140 ft. overall and with a beam of 34 ft., the largest centre-board yacht afloat, a fact which probably contributed to her downfall, although the prime cause was the shifting of moveable internal ballast. Lord Dunraven's view on ballasting was common throughout the nineteenth century and it was generally held that too much external ballast, i.e. on the keel, would cause a yacht to work itself to pieces. Alternative suggestions included the mounting of internal weights on springs to compensate for the motion.

Only relatively recently has the question of stability been properly explored. The Argentinian naval architect Juan Baader, writing in *The Sailing Yacht* points out that most merchant sailing vessels, save for the handful built in recent years for training purposes, have been basically unsafe, with the self righting moment diminishing from an angle of heel of 35–40 degrees. These vessels were representative of earlier tradition and practice. By comparison,

Major Tilman spent more time at sea aboard **Mischief** than on land during fourteen years of a most remarkable cruising partnership. Tragically, the partnership ended in 1968 when Mischief was lost off Jan Mayen.

(overleaf) The idea behind the 50/50 motor-sailer is that the advantages of the sailing boat and motor yacht are combined. In practice, the idea seldom works very well, and heavily engined motor-sailers rarely perform satisfactorily under sail. One of the most attractive and most successful of this breed is **Blue Leopard**, designed by Laurent Giles and partners.

Baader's curves for a modern ocean-going cruiser show her to be capable of withstanding an angle of heel of up to 72 degrees—an angle likely to be exceeded only in an enormous breaking wave crest.

Slocum's *Spray*, incidentally, rebuilt from an old hulk found on a New Bedford beach, had no external ballast. Nonetheless stability curves derived from drawings published in the American journal *The Rudder* show her to be theoretically uncapsizeable.

As indicated, racing has stimulated the design of sailing yachts. Lord Dunraven's philosophy is no longer valid, for *ocean* racing now holds sway and only the tiniest sailing craft can expect to remain in 'Smooth or comparatively smooth waters'. Dr Claud Worth, British eye specialist, founder-Commodore of the Little Ship Club, in 1926, and a luminary of the Royal Cruising Club, applied his scientific training and wide experience to the improvement of the sailing yacht and her gear. In the 1920s and 1930s, the Gaff rig was supplanted by the easier to handle and more efficient Bermudian rig, a long-standing sail plan which first drew widespread attention during the Olympic Games staged at Amsterdam in 1920.

Sophisticated equipment, e.g. the echo sounder in place of the cumbersome (and occasionally hazardous) leadline, has made the modern yachtsman's lot even easier. New building materials have appeared, some successful, some not. Glass fibre, though not immune to abrasion (and, alas, soluble in certain types of fire extinguisher foam) can be employed with advantage in craft of up to 500 odd feet, the currently regarded maximum, beyond which the physical problems increase. An American attempt to introduce stainless steel was thwarted by the discovery that the rivets, through being forged, assumed a slightly different position in the electro-chemical scale and that corrosion thus continued unabated. In developing the motor yacht, difficulties have attended the introduction of gas turbine propulsion, principally because of handling problems in confined waters; the 102 ft. gas turbine powered *Mercury* built by Vospers of Portsmouth for the Greek shipowner Stavros Niarches was only partially successful in this respect.

Today many cruising motor yachts are of the fast planing type. One recent British example is the 43 ft. 8 in. *Spirit of Ecstasy,* built for S. E. Macey by the Dorset Yacht Company in 1964 and with twin 400 h.p. Rolls-Royce diesels. A comfortable cruising yacht, she nevertheless came second in the 172-mile Daily Express Cowes-Torquay race of 1966 at an average

Eric and Susan Hiscock's **Wanderer III.**

of $35\frac{1}{2}$ m.p.h. In America fast 'houseboats'—in fact flat sided bungalows atop fast planing hulls—are a current phenomenon.

Beyond the widespread adopting of the Bermudian mainsail, experiments with rig have remained—experimental, though some progress has been made with a battened lugsail of the type used for centuries in China. Col. H. G. Hasler, introduced a sail of this type in his 26-ft. Folkboat, *Jester*, in the Single-handed Transatlantic race of 1960. Its considerable advantages in ease of trimming and handling almost compensated for certain drawbacks in

Long-range cruising has been facilitated by a number of innovations in the field of single-handed sailing. A leading innovator has been Col. 'Blondie' Hasler whose development of self-steering gear and experiments with unconventional rigs are well known. His unusual Folkboat, **Jester**, was evolved for the single-handed Transatlantic race.

efficiency and Hasler made a fast passage, spending much of his time engaged in carpentry or practising the clarinet, whilst other competitors fumbled about their decks in repeated sail changes.

Experimentation has extended to include the catamaran and trimaran, both of which have accumulated a mixed record. The advantage of both types—speed potential and a large deck space—are offset by the need for economy in weight and the consequent risk of disintegration in bad weather. Furthermore, instability sets in much earlier, and the wind acting under a hull lifted from the sea naturally adds to capsizing moment; witness the turning turtle of the large catamaran *Golden Cockerel* when being sailed hard, south of the Isle of Wight, in 1967. Today Piver-designed trimarans regularly traverse Atlantic and Pacific waters though designer Arthur Piver himself disappeared during a single-handed passage from San Francisco in 1968.

A much heavier cat, Dr David Lewis's *Rehu Moana*, successfully rounded the world, via the Straits of Magellan. She was, however, of a displacement type designed by Colin Mudie and advantageous chiefly in the accommodation she provided for Lewis and his young family. Her original double masted rig, tried on an incident-laden voyage to Iceland sponsored by 'The Guardian' newspaper in 1963, was found wanting. Because of the early stiffness of the type, and failure to heel before the wind, both spars and rigging must be of sterling stuff; on *Rehu Moana*, a more conventional cutter rig was found to do the job better.

The catamaran, incidentally, was reputedly under scrutiny in the reign of Charles II. Its long voyage of acceptance, as yet incomplete, reached a possible turning point with the construction of the 40-ft. *Manui Kai* in Hawaii soon after the Second World War. In Britain, G. Prout and Sons, of Canvey Island, are one concern which has developed a range of cruising cats; they built *Rehu Moana*. Their largest to date, the 78-ft. *Tsulamaran*, launched for Mr Patrick Hall in 1965 offers accommodation for 14 people and with two 100 h.p. Mercedes auxiliaries can cruise at 12 knots under power alone.

The record of the 'conventional', single hulled displacement yacht is a more secure one than that of the cat or tri. Capsizes in deep water have been mercifully rare and the number of recorded instances is few. The American racer *Dubloon* rolled over and righted herself while on passage up the Eastern seaboard. Better known still is the capsize in 1957 of the 46-ft. ketch *Tzu Hang* whilst running before big seas about 900 miles short of Cape Horn. The occupants, Brigadier Miles Smeeton, his wife Beryl and John Guzzwell, concluded afterwards that the yacht had been pitch-poled, i.e. turned end over end, a possibility for which it is difficult to make design allowances!

The incident is remarkable in several respects, not least the survival of Beryl Smeeton, who was hurled overboard and injured, and the sang froid of all three (Guzzwell, a skilled woodworker, after surveying the waterlogged, dismasted hulk, first sharpened his saw before commencing repairs). After refitting in Chile, the yacht was, incredibly, rolled over again, whilst running under bare poles. Hence the rueful title of Smeeton's book, *Once is Enough*.

On each occasion, however, *Tsu Hang* made port under jury rig. Guzzwell, not present for the second incident, subsequently completed a round the world voyage in the 20 ft. 10 in. *Trekka*, and later built, single-handed, another cruising yacht, the 20-ton *Treasure*. The Smeetons were similarly undeterred.

Cruising, of course, can take more modest and unspectacular forms, ranging right down, in terms of risk, to the new pleasure navy on the inland waterways in England. Here, despite the decrepitude of the canal system, adventure, coupled with a waxing enthusiasm for industrial archaeology, are inspiring interest in the canals and rivers of Europe, as yet relatively neglected by the pleasure boat. The Jersey yachtsman John Marriner, in his 54-ft. motor yacht *September Tide*, has covered the continental waterways extensively, and in addition to ocean cruises and coastal passages in the Mediterranean, has penetrated far up the Danube. One senses that his interest, a pioneering one in many respects, presages widespread growth for inland cruising. It is intriguing to note that the celebrated American yachtsman Irving Johnson, who has circumnavigated the globe several times, now has a new yacht *Yankee*—on the French canals.

Another modern trend, towards the 'motor sailor' or 50/50, emphasizes comfort rather than performance, though sailing characteristics of this type have improved greatly in the period since the Second World War. The very largest sailing vessels, such as Charles Nicholson's magnificent 699-ton three-master *Creole*, have been capable for a considerable time of carrying powerful engines without crippling sailing performance (*Creole*, built in 1937, can cruise at 11 knots under engine alone). In smaller craft, however, the weight of an auxiliary carries a premium and engines are not yet light enough for satisfactory sail and power characteristics in, say, an eight tonner operating in an offshore lop.

Some motor sailors make no bones about their identity. The latest *Southern Cross* for instance,

The **Ile de Feu**, reefed down in a good breeze.

2069

a magnificent vessel on the grand scale, has too high a bow and too full a hullform for top line sailing. All these characteristics though, add to the comfort and dryness of the vessel, while the power of her engines (two 230 h.p. Gardner diesels) and her extensive sail area, in addition to her sheer size (208 tons T.M.) ensure rapid progress even in tough weather conditions. *Southern Cross* was built by the Scottish firm of Yarrow and Co. in 1962 to the designs of W. MacPherson Campbell and to the order of Major F. W. Cundiff.

A cruising yacht is what you make it. Craft which qualify for the term 'great' are often quite humble in origin. The yachts, many of them tiny, which evacuated Dunkirk in 1940 are still remembered with affection, while a more recent example is the ex-pilot cutter *Mischief*. A far from pristine vessel, she can perhaps be most safely described as workaday,

When the armchair yachtsman dreams about his next cruising yacht, he dreams of **Creole** (left and right).

(left) Owned by Mr Stavros Niarchos, the three-masted **Creole** was designed by Charles Nicholson.

(right) Dr. David Lewis safely completed a circumnavigation of the world in his catamaran **Rehu Moana**.

yet she made some outstanding and even extraordinary voyages. Her owner, Major Tilman, an unusual combination of yachtsman and mountaineer, took her into both Arctic and Antarctic waters, principally in pursuit of previously unscaled peaks. In 1955 Tilman was awarded the Blue Water Medal of the Cruising Club of America, following his exploration of the Patagonian Channels. He visited Kerguelen, Baffin Bay and Greenland, where *Mischief* was trapped in the ice and suffered considerable damage. Conditions aboard were spartan (there was, for instance, a large tank fixed in the middle of the saloon) and the voyages were undoubtedly hazardous. Nonetheless, as Erroll Bruce has calculated, she sailed over 100,000 miles before she finally sank under tow in Arctic waters after grounding off Jan Meyan Island in 1968. Her crew survived.

Mischief lasted 62 years, although she was, as we might expect, somewhat the worse for wear towards the end. Her story is one of the incident and adventure that are the main hallmarks of cruising. 'Great' cruising yachts are, in the end, identified with great yachtsmen.

SIR THOMAS LIPTON

Single-Handed Sailing

WHEN ROBIN KNOX-JOHNSTON CAME ASHORE FROM HIS KETCH *Suhaili* AT FALMOUTH ON 22ND April 1969, he made single-handed sailing seem ridiculously simple. While astronauts were orbiting the world in hours, he had completed the first non-stop orbit by boat, a dull, dangerous and apparently masochistic voyage. He stepped on to the landing stage at the Royal Cornish Yacht Club and stamped his feet as they felt the firmness of land for the first time in ten months and three days.

He was cheerful, his beard neatly trimmed, trousers smartly pressed, his shirt freshly laundered. Sailors have crossed the Channel and looked in a much worse state. He faced a press conference, television cameras, barrages of questions and a crowd of thousands with good humour. He answered their questions eagerly and articulately. What kept him going? . . . The prospect of a good steak and a pint of beer. People, he said, were attaching a lot of importance to what he considered was a very nice holiday. He gave the impression that there was not a great deal of it. A sound boat, the ability to navigate, a lot of patience and anyone could sail round the world single-handed. But one close look at *Suhaili* was enough to dispel any thoughts that the voyage had been a pleasure trip. Her hull had been scarred and beaten by most of the world's oceans, her sails were stained and the old-fashioned style superstructure with its two owlish port-holes had cracked and shifted.

Knox-Johnston, a 30-year-old Merchant Navy officer, had features tanned the colour of ancient teak. Shaking hands with him was like patting the M.I. He deliberately underplayed the tremendous feat he had achieved; *Suhaili* really made the voyage. Anyone could have done it in that boat.

Robin Knox-Johnston is a tough man, mentally and physically. Exactly how dangerous it is to sail single-handed over great distances can be judged from the tragic disappearance of Donald Crowhurst, competing in the same Round the World race as Robin Knox-Johnston. Crowhurst's fast trimaran *Teignmouth Electron* was not caught in cyclonic winds or broken up by steep seas. From all the evidence it seems that Crowhurst simply slipped and fell overboard when he was not wearing a safety line. His boat, tuned to sail itself, did exactly that and vanished in the vast and lonely mid-Atlantic.

In an interview he gave before setting out on his round the world voyage Donald Crowhurst described a nasty moment sailing alone in the Channel 20 miles offshore. The wind got up and he went to take in a reef. He fell overboard, the yacht righted itself and he was only just able to climb back on board before it sailed away. There were no rails on board and he was not wearing a safety harness.

From the plotted course of *Teignmouth Electron*, Crowhurst seemed a certain winner of the £5,000 prize for the fastest non-stop circumnavigation in the Golden Globe Race. Then on 10th July 1969, the trimaran was found sailing empty off the Azores and after an examination of the logs on board it transpired that for the 243 days Donald Crowhurst was thought to be sailing around the world, he had never left the Atlantic. It was also clear that some of the radio messages sent giving his position were misleading and that towards the end of his voyage he was under considerable mental strain.

Geoffrey Williams' **Sir Thomas Lipton**, a trans-atlantic winner.

The mystery of Donald Crowhurst is surely the saddest story of single-handed sailing. It shows that behind the remarkable endurance of men like Knox-Johnston, Chichester and Alec Rose the danger lies not only in the sea but within the sailor himself.

In fact, Knox-Johnston was the only man to finish the Golden Globe Race and few more than half a dozen had considered attempting what Sir Francis Chichester described as the Everest of the sea. *Suhaili* was a rugged craft compared to some of her competitors and certainly built more in the spirit of Joshua Slocum's *Spray*, the first boat to sail around the world with a lone helmsman. Three sailors actually rounded Cape Horn and entered the Atlantic. Nigel Tetley was rescued when his trimaran *Victress* foundered in a force nine gale north of the Azores after nine months at sea. Bernard Moitessier, the extraordinary Frenchman who cared as little for the prize money as he did for the noise and demands of European life, was sighted first heading for the prize and next rounding the Cape of Good Hope. He had not made a mistake: he had decided to attempt a second world circuit and turned right allowing Knox-Johnston, a less mystical man, into the lead.

(above and right) Sir Francis Chichester's **Gipsy Moth IV** was specially designed for the solo circumnavigation by John Illingworth.

The difference between the two men is gulflike. Moitessier is seen as an ascetic, gaunt face framed in a wild mass of hair, lean muscular body locked in a yoga posture as his ketch *Joshua* ploughs along with steady winds. While he describes sailing in profoundly philosophic terms (when I sail, quite simply, I live), Robin Knox-Johnston thinks of other things. Someone promised him a parachuting journalist (female) as he neared the finish line. I hope, contemplated Knox-Johnston, she's on the pill.

Single-handed sailing is such a personal enterprise that the accounts written by men who undertake colossal voyages alone read with the kind of interest and incident attaching to someone newly released from a Trappist order of monks. The Walter Mitty dream of sailing one's own craft around the world is tremendously exciting theory but can be incredibly boring reality. It is impossible to describe the atmosphere to anyone who has not seen for themselves the terrifying curl of a mountainous sea from a small and fragile boat, a relative speck on the surface of some remote and angry ocean. How men react to the sight is something they may want to keep to themselves. What can they feel when the wind is so strong it flattens the waves and anything on them? Words are empty currency, a storm is a storm is a storm.

All they can do is dutifully to report to their sponsors: The wind was strong, the waves were big, I faced into them using only a staysail until they died down, then I carried on. Robin Knox-Johnston is perhaps the most deadpan of the circumnavigators: Bad weather? Yes, certainly. Depressed? Yes, from time to time when becalmed. Cold? Yes, it was cold, but the cabin was easy to heat. Frustrating? A little.

After ten months at sea he arrived within a few dozen miles of land but could scarcely make any headway against the choppy seas and currents. It took three agonising days to beat up Channel into Falmouth harbour, to hear the crack of the gun signalling the finish. But it was the crowds who were agonized, not Robin Knox-Johnston.

Waiting to meet him was that arch-adventurer and sailor Sir Francis Chichester, whose own home-coming to join the select band of solo circumnavigators to follow in the wake of Joshua Slocum was on 29th May 1967. Chichester was infected by John Masefield's 'Sea Fever'. His approach to a single-handed voyage around the world was spurred on by the thrill and spirit of the attempt and rested on considerable experience gained in breaking the single-handed transatlantic record with *Gipsy Moth III*. For Chichester to add a round the world solo to an adventure record that had involved many forms of transportation from bicycles to aircraft was remarkable. To do so at the age of 65 showed outstanding courage.

Chichester has never fought shy of publicity or of using publicity to provide the finance for his adventures. His autobiography contains a photograph of a fleet of veteran petrol tankers all bearing the sign Chichester used Shell Motor Oil and Spirit for his solo flight from London to Sydney, 1929–30. When he sailed around the world, *Gipsy Moth IV* carried the insignia for the International Wool Secretariat and Chichester blandly quaffed a considerable supply of Whitbread beer during the trip. With a specially designed yacht like *Gipsy Moth*, solo sailing demanded both courage and cash.

Chichester set out from Plymouth on a blustery day in August 1966. His outward course caught the North-East Trades past the Cape Verde Islands into the South-East Trades, around the Cape of Good Hope into the Roaring Forties to Sydney. The Forties carried him out to Cape Horn where several pressmen led dangerous lives trying to photograph the intrepid veteran. The rest of the voyage was spent smoothly, tacking and reaching up the Atlantic until the Westerlies could fill Chichester's sails and run him home to Plymouth, to a moving reception and a knighthood. The television channels were blocked nationally with news of his progress into harbour. For once yachting had become a mass spectator sport.

In comparison with Robin Knox-Johnston's easy handling of his press conference two years later, Chichester dealt with questions rather more bluntly. Perhaps the journalists were more obtuse. After four months alone you cannot expect me to make what you regard as sensible answers and these very abstruse questions make this even worse, he told them.

Why had he done it? Sir Francis rubbed his chin and replied there were 60 answers to that question, all of them correct but none could be fitted into a sentence. Yes, he had been terrified on one occasion when the boat rolled over. 'If you are in your bunk in the dark and the boat rolls over, it is quite sensational, I can promise you,' he said.

Gipsy Moth IV is a very large boat for one man to handle. Her dimensions were 49ft 9in overall, 38ft 5in waterline, 10ft 7in beam, 7ft 7½in draught, 854 sq ft sail area. Sir Francis needed the long waterline to maximise his chances of beating the time taken by the wool clippers to complete the Australia run.

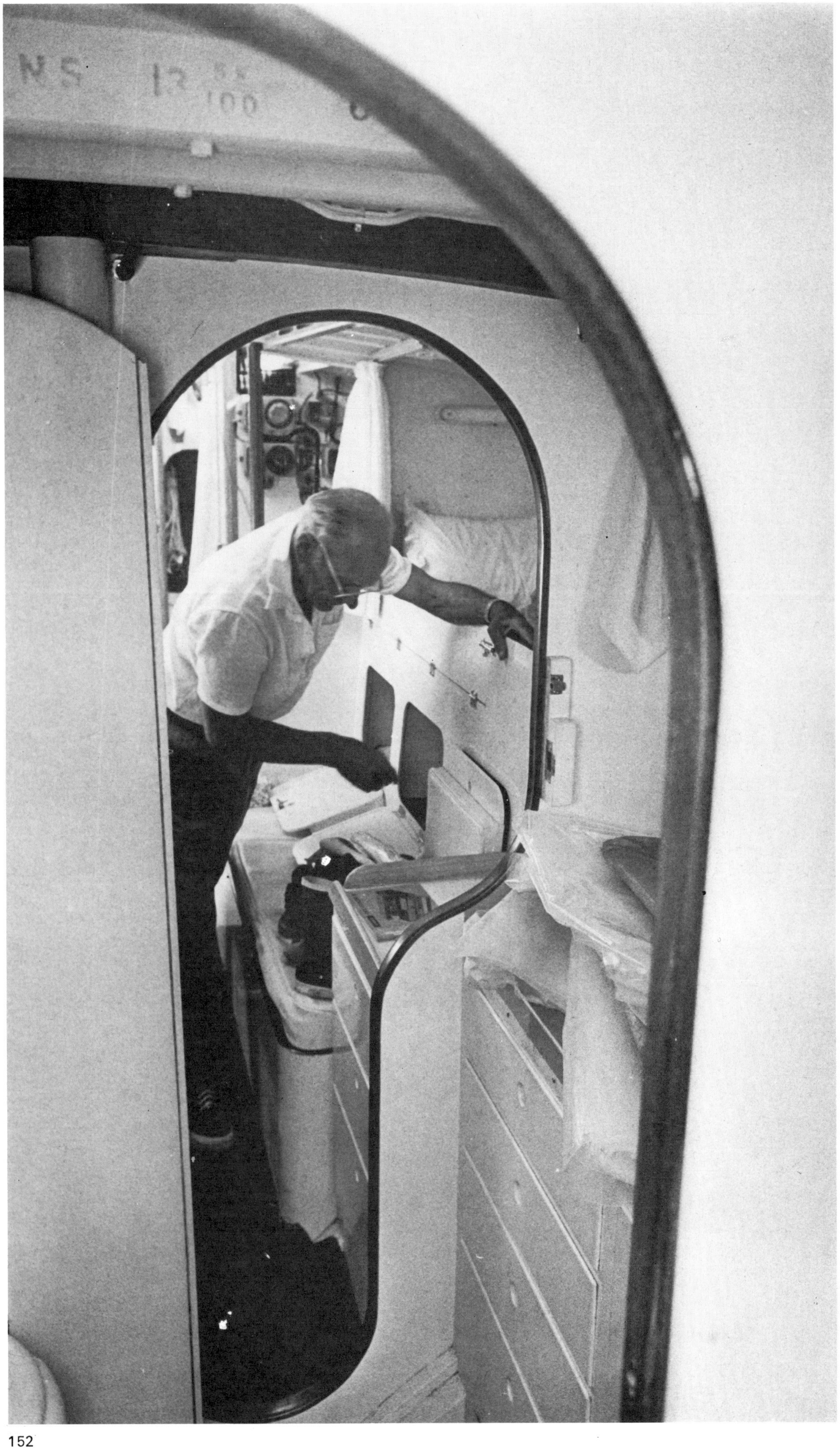

Sir Francis Chichester below decks on single-handed transatlantic record-breaker, **Gipsy Moth III.**

There had been mental strain. Solitude made him think more slowly as the weeks passed. Time began to lose its value but remained important enough to take navigational sightings to within a second. For him the voyage had intensified life.

The second man to receive a knighthood for his tenacity, skill and courage as a round-the-world solo sailor was a shy 59-year-old Portsmouth greengrocer, Alec Rose, whose ketch *Lively Lady* seemed a stoic tub set against the graceful lines of *Gipsy Moth IV*. She had two muscular wooden masts, a modest amount of canvas and a hull that went through waves like a meat cleaver through bone.

Rose, a close rival of Sir Francis Chichester in the 1964 solo race across the Atlantic, rejected all commercial backing. Nobody is on a percentage of anything. This is a very personal adventure I have saved for all my life, he said before he set out.

Rose was away from Portsmouth 354 days while his wife bravely continued to sell vegetables from their shop without trace of concern for her husband. He came back in July 1968 to cross the finishing line outside the Royal Albert Yacht Club in front of a huge crowd. The public once more were fascinated.

Alec Rose first set out in August 1967, intending to race Chichester around the globe. In the western approaches to the English Channel *Lively Lady* collided with a merchant ship, returned to Plymouth for repairs and added insult to injury by falling from the stocks in the dockyard. The collision meant he was unable to race Chichester, but Rose set sail undeterred as soon as his yacht had been repaired. His voyage caught people's imagination because it was made by such an 'ordinary' man, the greengrocer around the corner, without any financial backing.

Single-handed sailing has been facilitated by the development of self-steering gear, which enables the sailor to set a course to be held by his boat without further human intervention, provided the wind remains reasonably steady. There is little exact information about early methods of self-steering except that they probably date back to the very beginning of sailing.

One of the most wearisome aspects of prolonged periods at sea for a single-handed sailor in a small vessel lies in keeping everything in its place, not least oneself. Here, Sir Francis is safely tied to the telephone.

Paddles were used to steer the earliest boats and when these broke the craft became uncontrollable except by its sails. The Ancient Egyptians converted paddles into quarter rudders. In larger craft loss of one of these would not have been drastically important since the boats also carried large crews of rowers. But the inshore fisherman in his small boat must have found it necessary to steer by adjusting his sails in a certain way so that he could leave the helm to attend to his fishing. The reason why all sail-powered fishermen preferred boats with at least two sails is because they knew that to make a boat steer without a rudder is a relatively simple procedure of sheeting in the foresail and letting out the aft, causing the boat

Gipsy Moth III.

to bear away; reversing the operation will luff her. Self-steering with only one sail and no rudder is impossible.

The tradition was handed down and must have been well known to deep-sea sailors. Joshua Slocum, who set out to make the first round the world solo voyage in 1885 must have been able to make his yacht *Spray* self-steer while he was asleep. Heaving-to every night would have prolonged his voyage impossibly, as it was his 46,000-mile voyage lasted three years and two months.

Slocum was a ship's master and had experience of all kinds of ships and sail. Various of

Sir Alec Rose arriving in Portsmouth after his successful voyage round the world in **Lively Lady.**

his contemporaries on the East Coast of America had sailed across the Atlantic on their own. Howard Blackburn was notable among them. He had lost both hands through frostbite in winter off the Grand Banks of Newfoundland, when the boat from which he was fishing became separated from its parent ship. So the knowledge of self-steering when Slocum set out on his historic voyage was considerable. A sloop-rigged boat with the long, straight keel of *Spray* could be made to self-steer close hauled by sheeting in the jib tighter than desirable for maximum efficiency, freeing the mainsheet a few inches and fixing the rudder. Men like Slocum and Blackburn could go below and sleep while their craft ploughed on through the night.

On a free-running course, self-steering was also possible but required the jib to be sheeted flat amidships so that it acted more like a wind vane, pulling the head of the boat off the wind. With the mainsheet let well out there was a powerful luffing force from the mainsail which could not be neutralized by fixing the tiller to windward, because in a lull the boat would inevitably gybe. Slocum was a great experimentalist and reduced this gybing force by shortening the main boom and setting up a mizzen, to balance the boat close hauled and give the extra area. Nevertheless *Spray*, rigged as a ketch and sailing across the Pacific, still performed imperfectly running with the wind and, at Samoa, Slocum fixed a long bamboo pole as a flying bowsprit, on the end of which was set a flat-sheeted jib. Having made this modifica-

Robin Knox-Johnston, winner of the Golden Globe round-the-world race in **Suhaili.**

Bernard Moitessier aboard **Joshua** dropped out of the Golden Globe race when in a commanding lead. He set off round the world for a second time, finally coming to rest on a remote island in the Pacific. He is still there . . . Single-handed sailors are complex characters.

tion he set off again and during the 23 days it took to run the 2,700 miles from Thursday Island to Cocos Keeling Island, Slocum spent less than three hours at the helm, including the time it took him to beat into Keeling harbour. I just lashed the helm and let her go. Whether the wind was abeam or dead aft it was all the same. She always sailed her course. The steering jib, slicing the wind exactly down the middle, kept the bow pointing downwind, the ordinary foresail and main were pulling sails and his mizzen lay furled. Modern solo sailors with self-steering gear massed on the sterns of their yachts, like the innards of some outrageous clock, have wished they could have had the simple and trouble-free self-steering system of Joshua Slocum.

Joshua Slocum was a lean, darkly bearded man with cadaverous features usually sheltered beneath a broad-brimmed hat. Pictures of him reflect a man intensely introverted, driven to making voyages alone by grief. Slocum was close to his wife and built a boat, part dory part sampan, in which the couple sailed with their two sons from Paranagua, South America to Cape Roman in America, a voyage of 5,510 miles. It was not until he was in his forties and his wife had died, however, that he considered sailing around the world. He had run away to sea at the age of 14 and had been given his first command at 25. The books he wrote describing his adventures show him to be a thorough, thoughtful man for whom only the loneliness of the sea brought any real sense of peace.

Slocum's round the world sail began in March 1895 and ended in May 1898. Eleven years later, while sailing *Spray* alone on a voyage from Rhode Island to the West Indies, he

Voortrecker sailed from South Africa to England to compete in the 1968 transatlantic race.

disappeared. The Slocum Society in America is still active in publishing reports of single-handed voyages and perpetuating the spirit and art of solo sailing which Joshua Slocum established.

A host of sailors have followed Slocum, particularly in post war years, in helping to develop rigging and equipment for single-handed sailing. Eric Tabarly has been foremost among French yachtsmen in developing multi-hull craft for single-handed voyages over long distances. 'Blondie' Hasler originated The Observer Single Handed Race across the Atlantic in 1960 and has made four lone crossings in his 25 ft. yacht *Jester*. Recently Mrs Sharon Sites Adams became the first woman to sail the Pacific alone. Mrs Adams, a 39-year-old mother of two, sailed the 6,000 miles from Japan to San Diego in a 31 ft. ketch.

Other names associated with the solo Atlantic crossing are Bill Verity, a 40-year-old boat builder, who sailed from Florida to Ireland in a 12 ft. boat called *Nonoalca*. His 65-day voyage ended in July 1966. John Riding of Southport, Lancashire, crossed in 127 days in 1965 in an 11 ft. 6 in. boat called *Sea Egg*. Riding, a 6 ft. 4 in. man weighing over 25 stone, was half as long and half as heavy as his boat. The same year Robert Manry, an American journalist, crossed from America to England in 77 days in the 13 ft. 6 in. *Tinkerbelle*. Bernard Rhodes, a 24-year-old draughtsman from Barrow-in-Furness claimed a crossing from Las Palmas to Bridgetown, Barbados, in 19 days 22 hours 30 minutes in a home-made trimaran.

Nigel Tetley had to abandon his trimaran **Victress** in mid-Atlantic during the Golden Globe contest. The safety of multi-hulls at sea was again called into question.

Hugo Vihlen, aged 35, sailed over 4,500 miles from Casablanca in a 6 ft. boat and was only a few miles off the Florida coast when severe head winds forced him to abandon the crossing. His boat was called *April Fool*.

One of the most impressive and unsung exploits outside the Atlantic was Wolfgang Hausner's sail from Australia to Britain. Hausner, a 29-year-old draughtsman from Vienna completed the 22,500-mile voyage without self-steering gear, radio or engine. He bought the plans for his yacht in 1963 for £40 and worked in Australia as a crocodile hunter, sheep shearer and gold prospector to raise the money for his voyage.

Among the great characters of single-handed sailing was 75-year-old William Willis, another experienced sailor who disappeared without trace. In 1954 he drifted across the Pacific with a cat and a parrot in a home-made raft called *Seven Little Sisters*. Ten years later he crossed the Pacific again, on another raft called *Age Unlimited*. Next he turned his attention to the Atlantic. In 1967 a trawler rescued him when he ran out of food after covering 2,000 miles. He failed a second time and left Long Island on 1st May 1968, to attempt a third crossing of the ocean in his 12 ft. boat *Little One*. A Russian trawler found the boat adrift and empty 430 miles off Ireland. The oceans of the world may seem insignificantly small to the astronaut, or merely present him with a soft landing place, but to the lone sailor, they are vast, empty and always dangerous.

The Steam Yacht

STEAM TAKES UP CONSIDERABLY MORE SPACE THAN THE WATER FROM WHICH IT IS FORMED. The steam engine, therefore, functions on the principle of expansion. A fired boiler heats water and converts it into steam, which is carried to a cylinder where it drives first one piston and then another back and forth in the course of expansion. This action is converted into a rotational movement by means of a crank and flywheel which, through a connecting rod, revolves a shaft. The shaft can then be coupled to a propeller or a paddlewheel in order to drive a boat. The theory is a simple one but the equipment evolved for putting it into practice at sea was extraordinarily cumbersome.

Early steamboat machinery required mountains of coal to fire massive boilers, which produced brute force accompanied by clouds of thick black smoke. In short, the process was efficient but ungentlemanly. As a result, steam had almost completely taken the place of sail as a means of propulsion in the naval and mercantile fleets of the world, long before it came into extensive use in pleasure craft. Although the steam engine was heavy and dirty it could be relied upon to propel a cargo or a gunboat between ports without dependence on an unreliable wind. To yachtsmen, however, the vagaries of wind provided a challenge. Wind in the sails, too much of it or a lack of it, has to be mastered and provides a kind of muscle-yachting with hair on its chest, whereas mechanical propulsion, which enables the yachtsman to know that he will be back in time for tea, casts doubts on his virility.

It is interesting that British yachtsmen entered the steam yacht era in an entirely different frame of mind from that of their American counterparts. With a huge mercantile fleet, naval supremacy and a scattered Empire, the British were in an ideal position to lead the technical application of the steam engine, a British invention, to sea power. The manufacture of British marine engines was technically advanced by 1850 but, as a rule, British yachtsmen remained reluctant to employ steam propulsion in their yachts. There are exceptions to every rule and Mr Assheton Smith proved to be an exceptional yachtsman by commissioning the first steam yacht in 1830. For showing such initiative he was forced to resign his membership of the Royal Yacht Squadron but, undaunted by this social setback, he continued to commission another eight steam yachts before 1850. The Royal Yacht Squadron continued to regard the noisy, dirty engine with distaste and it was not until Queen Victoria had built two royal steam yachts (both called *Victoria & Albert* and launched in 1843 and 1855), that in 1856 it grudgingly permitted the ownership of steam yachts by its members. During the next thirty years, before the revolutionary change from sail to full mechanical power, the use of the auxiliary steam engine increased aboard large sailing yachts. The first part of the steam yacht era in Great Britain was largely confined to the production of these great auxiliary sailing vessels.

The invention of a suitable propeller persuaded many British owners to adopt auxiliary steam power, where even a small engine increased a sailing yacht's radius of action. Nevertheless, the auxiliary engine was strictly utilitarian and every effort was made to conceal its whereabouts. Owners contrived numerous ploys to hide the inevitable funnel; sometimes

Lord Brassey's auxiliary steam yacht **Sunbeam**.

it would be of very thin design, some would be portable and others hinged to be lowered out of sight when under sail. Mr Albert Brassey's *Czarina* was a typical product of this desire for secret steam yachting. *Czarina* was a 564 ton auxiliary schooner, designed by Benjamin Nicholson and launched in 1875. Her funnel was collapsible, in fact telescopic, and could be hoisted by a tackle from aloft. Albert Brassey, although fond of sailing in a fresh breeze, did not like being becalmed and as the wind died away the funnel would be hoisted quickly and the canvas stowed. If the breeze returned, sail had to be broken out again. This routine gave the crew plenty of sail drill and kept the engineer on his toes.

In America, yachtsmen were not nearly as cautious towards the steam engine. In 1853, when the steam yacht was still banned in English society, Cornelius Vanderbilt I of New York, the richest private citizen in the world (he was to leave an estate of $40,000,000 at his death in 1877), took delivery of America's first great steam yacht. There was nothing secretive about Vanderbilt's *North Star*. This floating hotel was massively constructed in oak by Jeremiah Simonson at a cost of $500,000 and measured 270 ft. long. Four boilers, each of them over 24 ft. in length, produced the steam to drive two 34 ft. diameter paddlewheels and to warm heaters in the yacht's ten staterooms. In the summer of 1853, Vanderbilt took *North Star* across the Atlantic to England, where, no doubt, both steam yacht and owner were met with the deepest suspicion by more traditional British yachtsmen.

North Star's maiden voyage from Sandy Hook to Southampton was completed in ten days, a remarkably short time for the Atlantic crossing in 1853. This achievement created a new concept of yachting which caught the imagination of American yachtsmen, although Vanderbilt's enthusiasm did not outlast his return to New York, where *North Star* passed immediately into commercial service as a passenger vessel.

America was emerging with great success from the years of hardship which had followed the War of Independence. Commercial tycoons like Vanderbilt had established private fortunes in excess of anything that the world had ever seen before. Having made money these men were not content to sit back to be blown about the sea in a sailing boat by the wind, their one desire was to get back to the office in order to increase their colossal capital assets. Their brains, of commercial genius, were directed towards speed and efficiency in the field of yachting. Their position in New York society was judged not by the number of hairs on their chests, or the length and vigour of the voyages they undertook out of office hours, but by the amount of money they made and the size of the yachts on which they spent it. During the second half of the nineteenth century, John Aspinwall commissioned over a dozen steam yachts while the tobacco heir, Jacob Lorillard, methodically ordered a new and larger steamer each season. Members of the New York Yacht Club were not only allowed to own steam yachts, they were expected to do so and anything under 150 ft. long was treated with contempt. The boys threw themselves into steam yachting with vigour; J. P. Morgan with *Corsair* (185 ft.), James Gordon Bennett with *Namouna* (227 ft.), William Astor with *Nourmahal* (232 ft.), and William Vanderbilt with *Alva* (285 ft.). In New York society a bigger and faster yacht was a better yacht but the best yacht of all was the most expensive. In his essay, 'American Steam Yachting', Edwin S. Jaffray wrote in 1886, 'There is a tide in the affairs of men which, taken at the flood, leads on to fortune. This tide is steam!'

While the smoke from American funnels grew thicker, blacker and more expensive, the key to an Englishman's status remained safely in the hands of the College of Heralds and although a short walk to the bank might precede the bestowal of a title, money was not generally discussed in society. The gentleman painstakingly concealed any connection between his commercial life and his leisure pursuits. Hence the rigmarole involved in concealing the funnel of the steam auxiliary engine aboard Albert Brassey's *Czarina*. Nevertheless, it was in this atmosphere that Albert's brother, Thomas Brassey, commissioned perhaps the greatest steam yacht ever to be launched, the *Sunbeam*.

Similar in profile to *Czarina*, the *Sunbeam*'s claim to fame can be judged on more than one level. As a cruising yacht she has never been surpassed in terms of distance covered and length of service to her owner. In the forty-two years of Thomas, later Earl, Brassey's ownership, *Sunbeam* logged 500,000 miles, including a famous circumnavigation of the world undertaken in 1876–7. She made further notable cruises to the West Indies and the U.S.A. in 1883 and again in 1892, to Calcutta and Bombay in 1893, to Australia, Tasmania and New Zealand

(above) Lord Brassey's brother Bertie's **Czarina**. A little unfair, perhaps, to have more than one in the family.

(below) Lord Brassey's exploits aboard Sunbeam inspired American Arthur Curtiss James to build **Aloha** for a round-world trip in 1910, when fully-rigged auxiliary steam vachts were being superseded by 100 per cent steamers.

from 1895–7, from Australia to England in 1900, to Canada in 1903, the West Indies in 1905, Iceland and Canada in 1910, Bombay in 1913 and India in 1916. During the First World War she served as a hospital ship in the Mediterranean. In addition she visited nearly all the cruising grounds of the British Isles, Scandinavia and the Baltic. It would be difficult for a yachtsman to anchor in a harbour today which has not been visited by the *Sunbeam*.

Sunbeam's circumnavigation was an achievement which excited the world. Lady Brassey's chronicle of the voyage, published after her return in 1877 sold millions of copies and passed into ten editions. Thomas Brassey writing in the *Times* of 2nd June 1877, gives us the bare facts.

'Sir,—Believing it possible that some interest may attach to the voyage completed on May 27 by the arrival of the *Sunbeam* at Cowes, I venture to offer to your readers a short narrative of our proceedings. The expedition is in some respects unprecedented; a circumnavigation of 35,400 miles has never before been made in the short period of 46 weeks, from which must be deducted 112 days of well-earned repose in harbour. We had, it is true, the advantage of steam, without which such a performance would have been an impossibility; but we travelled 20,517 miles under sail alone, and the consumption of coal has not exceeded 350 tons. The *Sunbeam* sailed from Cowes on July 6, called at Torbay, Madeira, Teneriffe, and the Cape Verde, crossed the line on August 8, and, carrying a favourable breeze in the south-east trades, arrived at Rio Janeiro on August 17. Following the coasts of South America, we visited Montevideo, Buenos Ayres, and Ensenada, steamed through the Straits of Magellan and Smyth's Channel, and reached Valparaiso on October 21.'

'While on the coast of Patagonia it was our privilege to rescue a crew of 15 hands from the barque *Monkshaven*, laden with an inflammable cargo of smelting coals, which had been on fire six days when we most providentially descried her signals of distress.'

'On October 30 we commenced our long and lonely voyage of 12,330 miles across the Pacific. We touched at Bow Island in the Low Archipelago, Maitea and Tahiti in the Society Islands, and Hawaii and Oahu in the Sandwich group. On January 21 we sighted Assumption in the Ladrones, and on the 29th arrived at Yokohama. While in Japan we were present at the opening of the railway from Osaka to Kioto by the Mikado, and subsequently cruised in the Inland Sea in severe winterly weather. At Simonoseki we found the people much agitated by the recent outbreak of the Satsuma clan. On February 19 we bade a reluctant farewell to Japan, and following the most direct route to England, visited in succession Hongkong, Canton, Macao, Singapore, Johore, Malacca, Penang, Galle, Colombo, Aden, Alexandria, Malta, Gibraltar, and Lisbon.'

Later in his letter, Brassey refers to the use of *Sunbeam*'s steam engine in the apologetic tones required of a British yachtsman in 1877.

'Of the total distance of 15,000 knots under steam, 12,000 were traversed under those special circumstances which seem to justify even a yachtsman in availing himself of the unromantic but invaluable engine.'

'The best run under steam alone was 230 knots, and the most successful continuous performance was on the passage from Penang to Galle, in the week ending April 15, when the *Sunbeam* steamed 1,451 knots, with a daily consumption of $4\frac{1}{4}$ tons of coal.'

'The best runs under sail from noon to noon were 298 and 299 knots respectively. The first was on the passage from Honolulu to Yokohama, sailing along the 16th parallel of north latitude, and between 163 deg. and 168 deg. 15 min. east. The second was in the Formosa channel.'

'The highest speed ever attained under sail was 15 knots in a squall in the North Pacific.'

Lord Brassey, the first yachtsman to pass the Board of Trade's examination for a Master's Certificate, describes his great yacht as 'a composite three-masted topsail-yard screw schooner, iron framed and with a teak skin-designed by Mr S. Clare Byrne of Liverpool. The compound engines by Messrs Laird, are of 70 nominal or 350 indicated horse-power, and developed a speed of 10·13 knots on the measured mile. The bunkers contain 80 tons of coal. The average daily consumption is four tons, and the speed eight knots in fine weather. The principal dimensions of the hull are:—Length overall, 170 ft.; beam, extreme, 27 ft. 6 in.; displacement tonnage, 531 tons. The sail area is 9,200 sq. ft.'

Sunbeam was not only a great cruising yacht but provided also a powerful example of the

The third and fourth **Corsairs**, both built in America for J. P. Morgan although American steam yacht owners generally favoured British designed and built boats.

advantages to yachtsmen of steam propulsion. At the same time she was capable of a satisfactory performance under sail, a point which she stressed by finishing sixth, with her screw removed, in the transatlantic race for the Kaiser's Cup in 1905, when, at the age of 31, she was competing with much newer yachts. Certainly in terms of size *Sunbeam* can be judged a great yacht, and even New York Yacht Club members would have appreciated her 170 ft. length. During her career she was visited by most people of any importance. It is safe to say that members of nearly all the ruling families of Europe and Asia walked her decks. The British Prime Minister, Mr Gladstone, recovered a loss of voice by cruising aboard *Sunbeam*, on doctor's orders. The poet laureate, Alfred Tennyson, asked irritably as he boarded her, 'May I smoke Everywhere'. An aggressive remark for a man who has just been loaned the use of a 500-ton schooner. The German Admiral Von Tirpitz chatted with Lord Brassey in the saloon on the eve of the declaration of the First World War. The Duchess of St Albans 'danced the hornpipe with our seamen with characteristic animation and activity'. Ambassadors, Consuls, Envoys and High Commissioners, however far from home they served, could not expect to escape from seeking out coal for *Sunbeam*'s boilers or from organizing mule-trains to carry the Brassey family to the interior for a look at the natives.

Cruising aboard the *Sunbeam* was as comfortable as could be expected with personal movement cramped by absurd Victorian clothes. Lady Brassey's one concession to yachting was to wear gumboots beneath her customary layers of petticoats. Otherwise, life at sea varied very little from life back home in Sussex. Fire broke out when a nurse heaped too many coals on the nursery grate during a cold night off Patagonia and, while sailing in the tropics, Lady Brassey was able to comment—'We had a service at 11.15 a.m. and again at 5.30 p.m. The choir has considerably improved.'

NOTE: Perhaps the clearest idea of Victorian cruising is given by reproducing the list of passengers and crew for *Sunbeam*'s circumnavigation.

Thomas Brassey, Esq., M.P. (Owner)	Hon. A. V. Bingham
Mrs Brassey	F. Hubert Freer, Esq.
Thomas Allnutt Brassey	Commander James Brown, R.N.
Mabelle Annie Brassey	Captain Squire T. S. Lecky, R.N.R.
Muriel Agnes Brassey	Henry Percy Potter, Esq. (Surgeon)
Marie Adelaide Brassey	
Isaiah Powell, Sailing Master	William Sebborn, A.B.
Henry Kindred, Boatswain	Walter Sebborn, A.B.
John Ridge Templeman, Carpenter	Turner Ennew, A.B.
Charles Cook, Signalman and Gunner	William Moulton, A.B.
James Allen, Coxswain of the Gig	Albert Wiseman, A.B.
James Walford, Captain of the Hold	John Green, A.B.
John Fale, Coxswain of the Cutter	Thomas Taylor, A.B.
Henry Parker, Second Coxswain of the Gig	
Thomas Powell, Forecastle Cook	Frederick Butt, A.B.
William Cole, Boy	Henry Tichenen, A.B.
Robert Rowbottom. Engineer	George Leslie, Steward
Charles McKenhnie, Second Engineer	William Ainsworth, Bedroom Steward
Thomas Kirkham, Leading Fireman	Frederick Parsons, Saloon Steward
George Burredge, Fireman	George Bassett, Second Saloon Steward
William Pride, Cook	Emma Adams, Nurse
Joseph Southgate, Cook's Mate	Harriet Howe, Lady's Maid
	Mary Phillips, Stewardess

Thus eight passengers were looked after by two naval officers and a surgeon who as gentlemen went along for the ride, supported by a paid crew of thirty-two.

(above) For many years royal yacht **Victoria and Albert III** headed the list of steam yachts in Lloyd's register of yachts, weighing in at 5,005 tons.

(below) Lord Brassey's circumnavigation in **Sunbeam** was far from single-handed. There were eight other passengers to talk to and a crew of 32 to look after them all.

G. L. Watson's first masterpiece was **Liberty**, which he designed for the American newspaper magnate, Mr Joseph Pulitzer. In wartime most large yachts were taken into service and Liberty acted as a hospital ship.

Of the steam auxiliary yachts, *Sunbeam* was undoubtedly the most remarkable but the largest was the Earl of Crawford's *Valhalla*. Built in Scotland by Ramage and Ferguson in 1892 to designs by W. C. Storey, *Valhalla* tipped the scales at 1,490 tons. She completed several long passages, notably finishing third, ahead of *Sunbeam*, in the Transatlantic race of 1905. After this achievement she was fitted out for a voyage of exploration. Sailing in November 1905, she visited South America, Ceylon and Madagascar, carrying mails for Tristan da Cunha en route and returning to England in May 1906. During this trip Lord Crawford carried out valuable research in oceanography and built up a remarkable collection of rare birds.

In America, the land of the one hundred per cent steam yacht, *Sunbeam* had a host of admirers. As late as 1910, Commodore Arthur Curtiss James was to build an auxiliary steam yacht with the intention of emulating the world cruise of Lord Brassey. His yacht was called *Aloha* and was built by the Fall River Company to the designs of Clinton Crane. *Aloha* was 180 ft. long overall, and carried a barque-rig with two powerful triple-expansion steam engines as auxiliary power. Her crew numbered some 38 hands.

By 1910, however, these vast auxiliary full-riggers had lost popularity both in America and in England in face of competition from the growing fleet of out-and-out steam yachts. Steam propulsion was, by then, accepted socially in England where the era of the pure steam-driven yacht began in about 1890 and continued until the beginning of the First World War.

When studying the slow change from auxiliary sailing yacht to pure steam yacht it is

The Duke of Westminster's **Cutty Sark** was built on the lines of a destroyer.

most noticeable that British designers were loath to depart from many of the sailing yacht features. Early steam yachts retained cutwater bows, long bowsprits and artistically designed counter sterns. The long overhangs fore and aft, the graceful sheer, the raked mast and funnel were all expressive of earlier sailing yachts.

American owners liked these somewhat outdated characteristics of British steam yacht design and commissioned a great many of their yachts from British designers. An added attraction to them was the lower cost of building British. In fact this advantage was nearly always lost because the Americans found that British steam engines were not fast enough and British plumbing positively uncivilized by American standards. This involved ripping out the interior of a new yacht on its arrival from Great Britain, in order to insert a faster American steam engine and more advanced plumbing.

British engines, although better engineered and more dependable, could not match the American article for speed. Nat Herreshoff, that remarkable American designer and yacht builder, was a leading developer of these fast steam engines. He progressed from the simple theory of a two cylinder compound engine to more complicated triple and quadruple expansion engines and even produced one with five cylinders in 1887.

By 1912 the pure driven steam yacht fleet had grown to an enormous size. With their mahogany, bird's eye maple and satin-wood panelling below decks, these yachts were the epitome of elegance and even in those days they could be owned only by the very rich. An owner could reckon that his yacht would cost him not less than one hundred pounds sterling per ton a week while in commission. Thus to run a vessel such as Sir Thomas Lipton's *Erin,*

Sir Thomas Lipton's **Erin**. A great sailing man's great steam yacht.

of over 1,200 tons, cost about £50,000 a year even before the First World War. The steam yacht had, at last, become the status symbol in Great Britain which it had been in America for over fifty years. Ownership of a steam yacht became a must for the idle rich and even richer, if not so idle, business tycoons of the Edwardian era—the bankers, industrialists and shipping magnates; the Tredegars, Inchcapes, Liptons and Selfridges.

Tycoonish symbols, however, were nothing compared to the symbols of monarchy. Queen Victoria had been one of the earliest patrons of steam yachting but towards the end of her reign, she complained that her old *Victoria & Albert II*, which had served her faithfully for nearly fifty years, was too small and quite beneath her dignity as Queen and Empress. In order to keep up with the Hohenzollerns and the Romanoffs she required, and was provided with, a steam yacht that was a thousand tons larger than any other royal yacht afloat.

Victoria & Albert III, launched in 1901, met with a mixed reception. One well-known nautical writer described the new royal yacht as: 'narrowly missing being the most beautiful steam vessel in the world. . . . She lacks a perfect symmetry, for all the nobility of her clipper bows and the graceful sweep of her sheer. The chief defect in her seems to be a certain ponderosity, although it is not easy to say exactly where she falls short of promise suggested at first sight.'

This diplomatic critic obviously felt that the *V & A* was horrible to look at. Her looks may have been an acquired taste, but her performance was unquestionably poor. Both

Marynthea was owned by Viscount Furness.

King Edward and King George V found her a bad sea-boat, difficult to manoeuvre. Nevertheless, *Victoria & Albert III*, at 5,005 tons, was not an object to be sneezed at. For years she headed the list of steam yachts in Lloyds register of yachts, ahead of the Czar of Russia's *Standart* (4,334 tons), the German Emperor's *Hohenzollern* (3,773 tons), and the Khedive of Egypt's *Mahroussa* (3,581 tons).

Of steel construction, *Victoria & Albert* was sheathed with wood over the greater part of her length and was believed to be the first vessel ever equipped with coaling ports cut in the sides. Internally the yacht was fitted out with care, being quite austere compared with the garish decor of other large yachts of her day.

Of the designers competing in the private rather than the royal yacht stakes, during these golden pre-war days of steam, G. L. Watson of Glasgow stood head and shoulders above the rest. He produced a string of magnificent vessels, of which two were masterpieces. He designed his first masterpiece, called *Liberty*, in 1908 for Mr Joseph Pulitzer, the American newspaper magnate. *Liberty,* constructed by Ramage and Ferguson at Leith, measured 1,571 tons, 250 ft. overall. Due to the idiosyncrasies of her owner, her design embraced some most unusual features. The bulkheads were as sound-proof as possible and during certain hours of the day when the owner was on board, no work was done at all, because random noises upset Mr Pulitzer intensely. The yacht contained a wonderful library but her owner seldom had the chance to use it for he seldom took a cruise. When his doctors ordered him to rest, it usually resulted in a few days spent aimlessly wandering about the Atlantic. Pulitzer would be accompanied by a horde of secretaries on these trips, while wireless kept him in touch with his newspapers. *Liberty* carried a special net to enable the ship's company to bathe free from sharks in the warm water of the Gulf Stream. This was among the few relaxations enjoyed in what was virtually a floating editorial office.

The second masterpiece to come from George Watson's drawing board was the *Sapphire*, built by John Brown & Co. on the Clyde in 1912 to the order of the Duke of Bedford. Measuring 285 ft. long overall and 1,421 tons, she was considered to come a very close second to *Liberty* in steam yacht perfection. The interior was strikingly decorated by the Duchess of Bedford, the walls being painted in high gloss white enamel with deep blue carpet fitted throughout. In every cabin a canary sang from a large and attractive cage.

Sapphire was bought in 1920 by Viscount Furness, an owner who juggled steam yachts like tennis balls. He had purchased, for the season of 1919, the 900-ton *Marynthea*, which had been designed in 1911 by Camper and Nicholsons. Having toyed with *Marynthea* for less than a year the ship-happy Viscount Furness sold her in order to purchase the more imposing *Sapphire*, complete with canaries, which kept him amused for fully three seasons.

There were drawbacks to steam propulsion, notably the mess of coaling and the smoke, which chased the ship when steaming downwind. But steam did provide the most flexible and the quietest form of machinery. When oil-burning boilers arrived, many coal-fired yachts were converted to oil fuel and their stokeholds enamelled white. But the introduction of the more compact marine diesel engine by Charles Nicholson in 1913 ended the popularity of the steam engine and few significant steam yachts were constructed after the First World War, although many of the pre-war titans continued in service.

G. L. Watson never really managed to progress completely from the traditional and grandoise scale of the pre-war steam yacht to the more aggressive and functional post war diesel yacht lines of which Charles Nicholson was the master. In 1930 he produced *Nahlin*, the last yacht to appear in the traditional steamer mould. She was one of the few yachts to be equipped with steam turbines, four of them, geared to two propeller shafts. *Nahlin* (1,574 tons) was built by John Brown & Co. for Lady Yule, the jute millionairess, and attracted notoriety when Edward, then Prince of Wales, chartered her for an Adriatic cruise with a company of friends, including the future Duchess of Windsor.

Another remarkable but more unusual British steam yacht of the same period as *Nahlin* was the converted destroyer *Cutty Sark*, owned by the second Duke of Westminster and built by Yarrow & Co. of Scotstoun in 1920, while in America the most significant post war steam yacht was the fourth and last *Corsair*.

The Morgan family were the most tenacious exponents of the steam yacht in the United States and had entered vigorously the American status steam yacht race of the late nineteenth century. They had always owned American built yachts and when many of their compatriots were placing orders on Clydebank in 1899, they had commissioned T. S. Marvel of Newburg, New York, to build for them the 1,936-ton *Corsair III*. In 1930 J. P. Morgan ordered a new all-American steam yacht at a time when American yachtsmen were abandoning steam in favour of diesel propulsion. *Corsair IV* was designed by Henry J. Gielow and built by the Bath Iron Works Corporation. Her power came from two steam turbines with electric drive, made by General Electric. At 2,181 gross tons, *Corsair IV* was a large yacht, particularly when one judges her size in relation to Mr Aristotle Onassis's *Christina*, the largest private yacht afloat today.

Of the two steam yachts built after 1940 *Christina* is the oldest. She was built in 1943 by Canadian Vickers Ltd. of Montreal as a freighter and is powered by two triple expansion steam engines. Originally christened *Stormont*, she was converted into a yacht in 1954 by Mr Onassis and registered at the port of Monrovia. One thinks of *Christina* as a huge yacht and it is easy to see the change of life in the world of huge yachts when one notes that with a gross tonnage of 1,526 tons, *Christina* is a clear 600 tons smaller than J. P. Morgan's *Corsair* built thirteen years earlier.

The other modern steam yacht is the British Royal Yacht *Britannia*, the only royal yacht to be built since the Second World War. *Britannia* was constructed by John Brown & Co. of Clydebank in 1953 to the design of Charles Nicholson. Four oil-fuelled steam turbines provide her power, coupled through single reduction gearing to twin screw shafts. Her steel

Nahlin

hull is electrically welded. Designed for conversion into a hospital ship in time of war, *Britannia* has an attractive profile. Her appearance, however, is extremely functional when compared with that of vessels like *Nahlin* and *Liberty*, which embodied the old concepts of steam yacht design.

Britannia and *Christina* are the last great steam yachts, their progress through the water is quiet and effortless to a degree which the diesel motor yacht cannot achieve. But with the trend towards smaller power yachts, the compact size of the diesel engine and the development of gas turbine propulsion aboard small boats it is unlikely that any more new steam yachts will be commissioned.

The Motor Yacht

THE IMPACT OF THE FIRST DIESEL POWERED YACHT IN THE WORLD HAD A MARKED INFLUENCE on the future of power yacht construction. The trouble with the steam engine was that with its stokehold and boilers it occupied a vast space, usually in the best part of the vessel. Quiet and flexible as the steam engine may have been, it was far too big. In 1913, the late Charles E. Nicholson conceived *Pioneer*, the world's first diesel yacht, in order to reduce space allocated to machinery.

In profile, *Pioneer* appeared to be an aggressive yacht, her lines resembling the trawler rather than the more conventional ornate steam yacht of a pre-war era. Built by Camper and Nicholsons on the south coast of England for Mr Paris Singer, *Pioneer* measured 163 ft. overall 24 ft. 6 in. in the beam, 9 ft. 6 in. in draught and 400 tons. She was engined by two Atlas Polar diesels, built in Copenhagen and developing 250 h.p. apiece. A shipside exhaust system was adopted and she carried no funnel in her first season, when more conventional yachtsmen than Paris Singer must have regarded her as a very odd sight. She carried 65 tons of fuel oil to provide a cruising range of 5,000 miles. At full speed, her fuel consumption averaged 26 gallons per hour, so that a conservative estimate of fuelling costs would work out at 6 shillings per hour, or under 6d. per mile. The corresponding consumption of coal under steam power would have cost at least four times as much, while the accommodation would have been reduced by 30 per cent.

After service in the First World War, *Pioneer* was purchased by the Crown Agents for the Colonies and drastically modified by her builders at Gosport, for use as the Governor's yacht in the Fiji Islands. She was equipped with saluting guns either side at the aft end of her forecastle head, permanent awnings, a research laboratory and a small prison. After years of service as a maid-of-all-work, tending the leper's colony and carrying a variety of small cargo, it was decided to scupper her at sea rather than to break her up.

Pioneer played a remarkable part in yachting history. Not only was she the forerunner of the modern motor yacht, but her construction in the south of England presented a challenge to the great Scottish yards, hitherto responsible for the majority of the great steam and sailing yachts. She was the first of thousands of yacht tons to be built in the south and her designer, many years later, was to build Britain's largest motor yacht.

The next remarkable diesel yacht produced by Camper & Nicholsons was the *Ara*, built in 1917 for the French Navy, being the only yacht in the First World War to mount the equivalent of two 6-in. guns. *Ara* was constructed on the lines of a sloop-of-war, with a slightly bulbous bow and a cruiser stern. Her measurements were 213 ft. on the waterline, 32 ft. on the beam and with a draught of 15 ft. and a displacement tonnage of 1,200 tons.

After the war, *Ara* was purchased by Captain Heriot and, while lying at Nicholson's yard, she was noticed by the American millionaire Mr William Vanderbilt. Vanderbilt was looking for a yacht and it was his intention to build if he could not find a suitable vessel. *Ara*, however, met his general requirements so well for type and size, that he decided to purchase her from Captain Heriot. The deal was completed in 1922.

The Norwegian royal yacht **Norge,** formerly Sir Thomas Sopwith's famous **Philante.**

Vanderbilt had the ship completely gutted of her accommodation to make way for a new layout. The original 860 h.p. Atlas diesel engines were replaced by larger engines of the same make, giving 1,200 h.p. each and a cruising range of some 7,000 miles at 14 knots.

Ara was equipped with a laboratory and tanks for the preservation of rare tropical fish. An electrically driven winch and drum housed two miles of wire cable for deep-sea dredging. Her navigational aids included a gyro-compass, an echo sounder and many other items which were novel at that time. Her radio was the most powerful available and, at breakfast, the world news was provided by a newsheet named the Ara Auditor.

Vincent Astor was another American yachtsman to commission an outstanding diesel yacht in the twenties. His *Nourmahal*, the second Astor yacht of that name, was designed in 1928 by Theodore Ferris of Cox & Stevens Inc., and was powered by two 6-cylinder Sulzer diesel engines rating 714 nominal horsepower. In line with many other American yachts of the time, she was constructed in steel by a German yard, F. Krupp, Germania Werft, at a price that was considered to be cheap in America. For a bargain $600,000 the thrifty Mr Astor acquired 1,969 gross tons and 264 ft. of the finest motor yacht afloat in American waters. President Roosevelt was a frequent and famous guest aboard *Nourmahal*, although the secretive, moody Vincent Astor spent a great deal of his time cruising aboard his mammoth yacht without family or guests, brooding in solitude on the best way to spend his money. On the outbreak of the Second World War, Astor sold *Nourmahal* into service with the U.S. Coast Guard.

In England, Camper & Nicholsons continued to dominate the market in luxury diesel yachts, which they had pioneered before the First World War.

Britain's other leading exponents of luxury yacht design, G. L. Watson of Glasgow, found it difficult at first to adapt themselves to diesel propulsion and the increasingly functional appearance of the new diesel yachts. The Watson-designed steam yachts, *Liberty* and *Sapphire* had dominated the glorious pre-war era of gilded figureheads and clipper bows. As late as 1930 Watsons were turning out steam yachts, like *Nahlin*, in the old mould. Even their diesel yachts retained the outdated characteristics of the pre-war steamers, although some would judge that a yacht like *Virginia* embodied the best principles of the new and the old styles.

Virginia was designed by Watsons and built by William Beardmore & Co. for Major Stephen Courtauld, the textile magnate, in 1930. Outwardly resembling a steam yacht, with clipper bow, long overhanging stern and masts, *Virginia* was powered by two 600 b.h.p. Sulzer diesels which gave her a maximum speed of 13·8 knots and enabled her to cross the Atlantic at 12½ knots without rebunkering. *Virginia* measured 209 ft. overall, 29 ft. 6 in. on the beam and 712 tons. Major Courtauld virtually lived aboard her for many years, cruising all over the world.

In 1937, that great British yachtsman, T. O. M. Sopwith, commissioned, from Camper & Nicholsons, one of the largest and most luxurious motor yachts ever to be constructed. The new yacht was called *Philante*. In size *Philante* was a match for Vincent Astor's *Nourmahal*, measuring 263 ft. overall, 38 ft. on the beam and 1,628 gross tons. A double bottom with a depth of 4 ft. was integral to construction throughout the ship's length. Her diesel engine developed 3,000 b.h.p. and provided a cruising speed of 14 knots over a range of 7,000 nautical miles. Undoubtedly, *Philante* could claim to be the best equipped yacht afloat in the world.

Working through the accommodation from bow to stern, *Philante*'s forecastle housed 16 crew, after of which came cabin space for 18 junior officers and stewards. Next came the sick bay, the carpenter's shop, the linen room, the store room and a cold chamber of 1,220 cubic feet capacity. The 50-ft. long engine room was placed amidships in front of three maids' cabins. The galley measured 23 ft. by 15 ft. and contained both oil-fired, solid fuel and electric cooking ranges; the best of all worlds. At the after end of the forecastle deck, a steel-lined store room was provided to house the racing sails, ropes, blocks and tackle needed by Tommy Sopwith for his J class and 12 Metre yachts. A gymnasium completed what an estate agent might describe as the 'usual offices'.

Philante's living accommodation was divided into a master stateroom, eight guest cabins and five saloons. The lower cabins gave 7 ft. 9 in. of headroom, 7 ft. 6 in. in the dining and smoking rooms and 8 ft. 10 in. elsewhere. The living room (13 ft. × 25 ft.), contained a fireplace

Shipping magnate Basil Mavroleon's **Radiant II** was built at his own yard in Sunderland at an estimated cost of £400,000. In every way an up-to-date motor yacht in a technological age, her size and furnishings reflect the spirit of an age now dead.

and mantelpiece; the ceiling forming a dome at each corner. An archway at the after end of this saloon led to a sitting room (12 ft. × 21 ft.), with double doors opening to the after deck.

The dining room, decorated in Adam style, was 30 ft. long and 22 ft. wide with steel-framed french windows at each end.

Period decoration was employed only in the dining room and the owner's state room, the latter being 'Old Spanish'. Predominating features throughout *Philante* were the rough, stone-like walls and leather-covered doors fitted with heavy wrought-iron door furniture. The smoke room was panelled in weathered oak and the corridors, vestibules and living rooms in American walnut. Eighty radiators were concealed in the panelling. A master clock controlled thirty-seven other clocks throughout the ship. The radiogram in the sitting room fed thirteen extension speakers, but a single grand piano was regarded as sufficient.

In the Second World War *Philante* was requisitioned by the Royal Navy and armed to

serve as an auxiliary vessel, covering 150,000 miles on active service. In 1946 she was purchased by the Norwegian nation and presented to their King Haakon VII, when she underwent an extensive below-deck conversion to fit her new role as the Royal Yacht, *Norge*.

The thirties saw a succession of these vast motor yachts like *Philante* and *Virginia*. It was an age primarily of space and luxury. Many sailing yachtsmen looked upon the great steam and motor yachts as 'gin palaces', holding them to be unadventurous and even unnecessary playthings of rich men who rarely knew one end of a boat from another. Such an outlook is both prejudiced and unfounded. The introduction of mechanical propulsion is probably one of the most important developments in the whole of yachting history, providing much needed auxiliary propulsion for sailing craft, and producing an entirely new branch of the yachting world—one which continues to develop. It is significant that some of the greatest yachtsmen and sportsmen that the world has seen, men such as Sir Thomas Lipton, Mike Vanderbilt and Tommy Sopwith, who devoted much of their lives to the sport of sailing, also owned some of the most advanced and the largest 'gin palaces' of their day. Many of these giants of the thirties are afloat and still giving first-class service.

In 1929 Camper & Nicholsons designed and built *Sister Anne* for the Hon. Mrs Reginald (Daisy) Fellowes, heiress to the Singer Sewing Machine fortune. *Sister Anne* was not in the league of giants, measuring 130 ft. overall with a gross tonnage of 230 tons. Nevertheless, this remarkable vessel has survived a long career. The 1969 edition of Lloyds Register shows that she is still in commission, owned by the Vega Corporation and based at Cannes. Remarkably, she still retains her original, single-acting Gardner oil engines after forty years of service and continues to be maintained to Lloyds 100 A.1. classification, the highest form of construction classification in British shipbuilding, which is subject to periodical survey during a vessel's life. *Malahne* is another design from Camper & Nicholsons and was built at their Gosport yard in 1937. Today she is registered in Lloyds with her original M.A.N. 6-cylinder oil engines. After thirty years she also retains her Lloyds 100 A.1. classification.

The 457-ton *Malahne* was built for Mr W. L. Stephenson to give a maximum speed of 15½ knots. She had a crew of eighteen, and her interior was decorated with customary verve, the owner's bath and washbasin being notable for their rich strawberry colour. *Malahne* was fitted with Hyland hydraulic steering gear and was equipped with the most up-to-date navigational aids. On leaving for a first voyage to the Mediterranean her skipper made the somewhat cryptic remark: Well, if we do not have a good time, it will not be the ship's fault.

Perhaps even more remarkable than the splendid record of *Malahne* is that of *Shemara*, built for Sir Bernard Docker in 1938. This diesel yacht, measuring some 835 tons and 212 ft. overall length, was designed and constructed by J. L. Thornycroft and Co. Ltd. of Southampton. *Shemara* is not only maintained to her original 100 A.1. Lloyds classification in the 1968 Register of Yachts, retaining her original Atlas Polar engines, but she is registered in the name of her original owner. Sir Bernard Docker has cruised *Shemara* for thirty years, always maintaining and modernizing her equipment to first-class standards. It has been one of the most successful partnerships between a great yacht and a great yachtsman in motor yachting history. The original definition of a yacht is that it is a vessel used primarily for pleasure purposes, *Shemara* is a great yacht indeed in terms of the pleasure she has afforded her owner for thirty years. In August 1968 this partnership ended when Sir Bernard Docker sold *Shemara* to the London Property dealer Harry Hyams, for a reputed price of £240,000.

These are all vast yachts, often considered 'great' because of their size, the efficiency of their equipment and the character of their owners. It will be remembered that in the nineteenth and early twentieth centuries, sailing yachts, the schooners and first-class cutters, were judged in precisely the same fashion. Indeed, the development of the older sailing and the younger, mechanically powered, departments of the sport have followed a similar course.

Since the First World War, the tendency has been for both sailing and power yachts to be smaller, while the emphasis is on maximum possible speed on a reduced waterline length, and increased seaworthiness. The object has been, and continues to be, the provision of fast, safe and easily-handled craft, either under sail or power, suitable for use by a wider public in an increasingly affluent society. Today yachting has become a popular sport with one of the fastest growth rates in the world. It has ceased to be the sport of the rich man, and America has been largely responsible for this emancipation. The Americans also pioneered ocean

(above) **Sister Anne** was built at Camper and Nicholson's in 1929. Today she is still in service and still registered 100 A.1. at Lloyd's.

(below) **Pioneer**, the world's first diesel yacht, designed by Charles Nicholson for Mr Paris Singer in 1913.

The shape of things to come. **Cohete,** designed by Renato Levi. Tomorrow's Great Yachts will be relatively small and capable of high speeds.

racing, which apart from dinghy sailing, has become the popular mainstay of yachting. Similarly, they have pioneered offshore racing for powerboats, a new branch of the sport which has radically changed the development of modern power yachts.

Since the Second World War, power yachting has reflected increasingly the demand for speed with safety at sea. An identical demand led to the development of ocean racing. But before that, as early as the 1890s, the American Charles Pryer could write:

'Of late years the steam yacht has almost entirely disappeared from American waters, to give place to the naphtha launch and it looks now as though this craft in turn could be superseded at no distant date by the electric motor.' With the imminent development of fuel cells, this latter hope must be re-echoed, some 70 years later.

Pryer notes that for larger craft, steam still held its sway and that some steam yachts could attain an almost incredible speed, the maximum being over 30 knots. This seems an exaggeration, although for a long time the best recorded speed made under power stood at 34·5 miles per hour, achieved in 1897 by Sir Charles Parson's 100 ft. steam turbine vessel, *Turbinia*. During the first half of the twentieth century the world water speed record was sought by American and British enthusiasts such as Gar Wood, Sir Henry Seagrave and Sir Malcolm Campbell. There were speedboat races too, mostly in America, such as the Detroit Gold Cup. But speedboat races and the world water speed record had little influence on the development of the motor yacht, which, as we have seen, continued to be large, comfortable and relatively slow.

Greek Tycoon Stavros Niarchos's **Mercury**, the world's first gas turbine yacht, is based on the Brave class fast patrol boats of the British Navy and is capable of over 50 knots.

In the mid-1950s the American sportsman, Sam Griffith, pioneered the sport of offshore powerboat racing, and this has had great effect on motor yacht design in a comparatively short time. Griffith became the greatest name in post war powerboating, winning almost every major event as well as achieving the world water speed and endurance records. In 1956 it was Griffith who organized the first Miami–Nassau race. During the next decade the sport grew unimpeded, although Griffith was to die in 1963. In 1961 Sir Max Aitken organized the first 180-mile Cowes–Torquay powerboat race, which has become an annual event in Britain. By 1967 a World Driver's Championship had been set up covering races in the States, the Bahamas, France, Italy, Sweden and Great Britain. Powerboat racing, like ocean racing, had come to play an important part in the international yachting calendar. Despite the groans of the out-and-out sail men, distinguished sailors like Dick Bertram and Sir Max Aitken led the early development of powerboat racing.

Powerboat racing, following the requirement of speed with safety, saw the innovation of techniques in hull design, engine installation and provision for safety equipment which have been applied to advanced motor yachts outside the field of racing. The American designer Ray Hunt developed the 'deep V' hull form, where the hull assumes a 'V' shape, through from bow to stern instead of 'veed' at the bow and flat at the stern as it used to be. It was found that the 'deep V' went a long way in solving the problem of the more conventional hull form, planing at high speed, which buffeted and crashed from wave to wave. The new deep V produced a smoother and consequently safer ride. Sam Griffith's famous *Blue Moppie*

Mr Vincent Astor's **Nourmahal** was built in steel by Krupps in Germany.

was one of the most successful Ray Hunt-designed powerboats. The deep V hull formula was adopted aboard *Philante V*, a high-speed yacht measuring 117 tons, capable of maintaining speeds approaching 20 knots and built by Camper & Nicholsons for Tommy Sopwith (Junior) in 1961.

In Italy, the marine architect Renato Levi has developed on the deep V with his Delta Configuration, where the hull form appears wedge-shaped when seen in plan and profile. The British powerboat *Surfury*, designed by Levi and owned by Charles and Richard Gardner, is the most successful product of Delta Configuration to date. Levi has applied his high-speed hull form to larger motor yachts. In 1964 he designed the 80 ft. high-speed motor yacht *Cohete* for a Panamanian company.

In many respects *Cohete* is a revolutionary yacht. Her hull was constructed in light alloy by Cantiere Rodriguez, an Italian yard which specializes in the alloy construction of hydrofoil passenger craft. Peraluman AG4 was the material used and the construction was part riveted, part welded, the use of Linde welders enabling a continuous weld. *Cohete*'s hull plating varies in thickness between 6 mm. on the bottom and 5 mm. for her topsides. She is powered by twin C.R.M. diesels developing 1,050 h.p. and carries 13 tons of fuel. She has a displacement of 60 tons and is capable of a maximum speed of 24 knots, with a continuous cruising speed between 18 and 20 knots. Levi has this to say of her design: I would describe the hull design as of a moderate deadrise. Before commencing construction, approximately

Ara started life in the French navy, and was converted into a yacht by Mr William Vanderbilt in 1922.

three months' tank testing was done, which revealed some interesting data on the position and usefulness of the six longitudinal risers which are fitted on the bottom and which extend to the transom of the vessel.

The application of these longitudinal risers, otherwise known as spray strips, is a Levi speciality. Their object is to break up and deflect the water on which the boat is travelling, thus reducing the wetted area of the hull and increasing its efficiency at speed.

Incorporating techniques which have been discovered through powerboat racing, *Cohete* maintains standard of accommodation and comfort which would not be out of place aboard a larger, slower and more traditional power yacht. She can sleep twelve guests and four crew. The six guest cabins are all provided with their own bathrooms. There is a laundry and a well-fitted kitchen, complete with electric stove, twin frigidaires and a deepfreeze. The navigation aids include an automatic pilot and radar, while there is provision on the after-deck to carry a launch and a small motor car.

In Britain, Commodore Peter Du Cane of Vosper Ltd., for a long time one of the world's leading authorities on high-speed hull design, has done more than anyone perhaps, to develop the fast motor yacht.

Vospers had developed the Brave class fast patrol boat for use with the British Navy, powered by gas turbines and capable of over 50 knots. In 1960 Vospers produced the world's first power yacht to carry no form of piston engine. This was the *Mercury*, designed by Du

At present owned by London property man Harry Hyams, **Shemara** was built in 1938 and served her first owner, Sir Bernard Docker, for thirty years.

Cane for Mr Stavros Niarchos and based on the Brave class patrol boat. *Mercury*, measuring 102 ft. overall length, recorded 54 knots during her initial trials in February of 1961.

The basic Brave class hull was used in *Mercury*'s construction, fused with an interesting superstructure made up of glued wood laminations, protected with a coating of resin-glass. The hard chine hull was made up of glass sheathed mahogany planking (double diagonal), over an aluminium alloy frame. Triple screws were driven by three Bristol Siddeley gas turbine engines, developing 3,500 b.h.p., maximum power; to 2,800 b.h.p., continuous rating. The auxiliary machinery consisted of two Rover gas turbine generating sets.

Mercury was, and still is, a very advanced yacht. There were problems in designing a yacht for comfortable cruising over 400 miles at 46 knots. Sophisticated soundproofing of the engine room was required to reduce the engine noise to a level similar to that experienced on board a modern jet airliner.

A.E.G. steering motors of the electro-hydraulic vane type were installed, one integral with the stock of each of the three rudders, connected to the steering position by electric cable. However, the problem of steering a gas turbine boat of such a size in confined waters was never completely solved. *Mercury*'s high cavitation propellers were developed by Vospers in conjunction with the Admiralty.

In 1962, Commodore Du Cane designed *Tramontana*, which won the 196-mile Cowes–Torquay powerboat race for Dick Wilkins at an average speed of 32 knots. In 1965, Du Cane's own 52 ft. waterline length, *Diamarcha* appeared. With a hard chine hull developed

Philante (now **Norge**) was built by Camper and Nicholson's for Sir Thomas Sopwith in 1937. One of the most luxurious diesel yachts ever built, a double bottom with a depth of four feet was integral to construction throughout her length.

from *Tramontana, Diamarcha* cruises between 16 and 19 knots, powered by twin G.M. diesels set aft. Her steering is controlled by buttons rather than wheels and her navigational equipment is of the most advanced.

Although the tendency in motor yacht design is towards the relatively small and fast, there are a few motor yachts of considerable size still being built. In some ways such yachts as *Radiant II* and Henry Ford's *Santa Maria* are similar in concept to *Virginia*, Major Courtauld's yacht of the thirties, which employed the new diesel propulsion in the elegant if outdated hull and superstructure of steam yacht days.

Built by Basil Mavreleon at his Austin & Pickersgill yard in Sunderland, *Radiant II* was completed in 1961. At 680 gross tons, *Radiant II* is an uncommonly large motor yacht with a crew to passenger rating of 2 to 1 (24 crew, 12 passengers) and seven bathrooms. This pre-war aspect tends to obscure the fact that she is in every way a thoroughly modern yacht, bristling with radar, stabilizers, automatic pilots and air conditioning. Henry Ford's *Santa Maria*, built by C. Van Lent in Holland in 1963, measures 183 tons and is similar, if smaller, to *Radiant II*. But it seems that this breed of vast motor yachts is finally dying out, just as the great cutters, the schooners and the J class sailing boats died.

With the development of high-speed hull design, and with new thinking in terms of propulsion (perhaps nuclear and certainly gas turbine), the great motor yacht of the next decade will most likely measure between 50 and 100 feet, and be capable of sustained cruising speeds in excess of 30 knots.

Surfury, designed by Renato Levi, shows her V-shaped hull formation. The relatively new sport of offshore powerboat racing develops design thinking with regard to motor yachts in much the same way as ocean racing influences cruising yacht design.

The 457 ton **Malahne** was built for Mr W. L. Stephenson in 1937. She is still in service.

Appendix 1: Yacht designers

Name	Nationality	Great Yachts
Anker, J.	Norwegian	Dragon Class (1929)
Austin & Pickersgill	British	M.Y. *Radiant II* (1961)
Burgess, W. S.	American	*Nina* (1928) *Rainbow* (1934) *Enterprise* (1930) *Ranger* (1937 with O. Stephens)
Byrne, St C.	British	*Sunbeam* (1847)
Canadian Vickers Ltd	Canadian	S.Y. *Christina* (1943)
Carll, D.	American	*Vesta* (1866)
Crane, C. H.	American	S.Y. *Vanadis* (1908) S.Y. *Aloha* (1910)
De Voogt, H. W.	Dutch	M.Y. *Santa Maria* (1963)
Du Cane, P.	British	M.Y. *Mercury* (1960) M.Y. *Tramontana* (1962) M.Y. *Diamarcha*
Ferris, T. E.	American	M.Y. *Nourmahal* (1928)
Fife, W.	British	*White Heather* (1907) *Shamrock* (1908) *Hispania* (1909) *Vanity* (1923) *Cambria* (1928)
Fox, U.	British	*Avenger* (1927) *Coweslip* (1962)
Gardner, W.	American	Star Class (1911)
Gardner & Cox	American	*Atlantic* (1903)
Gielow, H. J. Inc	American	S.Y. *Corsair IV* (1930)
Herreshoff, N. G.	American	*Navahoe* (1893) *Vigilant* (1893) *Westward* (1910) *Resolute* (1914)
Hunt, C. R.	American	*Blue Moppie* (1959) M.Y. *Philante V* (1961 with Camper & Nicholsons Ltd)
Illingworth, J.	British	*Gipsy Moth IV* (1966) *Sir Winston Churchill* (1966 with Camper and Nicholsons)
Levi, R.	Italian	*Surfury* (1965)
Mudie, C.	British	*Rehu Moana* (1969)
Nicholson, B.	British	*Czarina* (1877)

Name	Nationality	Great Yachts
Nicholson, C. E.	British	S.Y. *Sagitta* (1908) S.Y. *Miranda* (1910) S.Y. *Marynthea* (1911) M.Y. *Pioneer* (1913) *Shamrock IV* (1914) M.Y. *Ara* (1917) *Mouette* (1928) M.Y. *Crusader II* (1929) M.Y. *Sister Anne* (1929) *Endeavour* (1934) *Bloodhound* (1936) M.Y. *Philante V* (1937) M.Y. *Malahne* (1937) *Creole* (1927)
Nicholsons (Camper & Nicholsons Ltd. have also been responsible for)		M.Y. *Philante V* (1961) *Quiver IV* (with C. R. Hunt) *Sir Winston Churchill* (1966 with J. Illingworth)
Oertz, M.	German	*Meteor IV* (1909) *Meteor V* (1914)
Payne, A.	Australian	*Gretel* (1962)
Piver, A.	American	Pioneer of multihull yachts
Prout, R.	British	*Tsulamaran* (1965)
Ratsey, M. E.	British	*Cambria* (1868)
Rhodes, P. L.	American	*Carina* (1955) *Weatherly* (1958)
Rouse, H. S.	British	*Tzu Hang* (1939)
Scott & Co.	British	S.Y. *Erin* (1896)
Soper, J. M.	British	*Satanita* (1893)
Steers, G.	American	*America* (1851)
Steers, H.	American	*Henrietta* (1861)
Stephens, O.	American	*Dorade* (1930) *Stormy Weather* (1934) *Ranger* (1937 with Starling Burgess) *Vim* (1939)
Storey, W. C.	British	*Valhalla* (1892)
Thorneycroft & Co.	British	M.Y. *Shemara* (1938)
Vandeusen, J.	American	*Fleetwing* (1865)
Van Essen, U.	Dutch	Flying Dutchman Class (1957)
Watson, G. L.	British	*Thistle* (1887, *Meteor I*) *Valkyrie II* (1893) *Britannia* (1893) *Valkyrie III* (1895) *Meteor II* (1896) S.Y. *Margarita* (1900) S.Y. *Liberty* (1908) S.Y. *Sapphire* (1912) S.Y. *Nahlin* (1930) M.Y. *Virginia* (1930)
Webb, J. B.	American	S.Y. *Corsair III* (1899)
White, Sir W. H.	British	R.Y. *Victoria & Albert* (1899) *Terpsichore* (1920)

Appendix 2: Yacht builders

Name	Nationality	Great Yachts
Astilleros Karrard	Spanish	*Hispania* (1909)
Bath Iron Works Corp.	American	S.Y. *Corsair IV* (1930) *Ranger* (1937)
Beardmore & Co.	British	M.Y. *Virginia* (1930)
Bertram, R.	American	*Blue Moppie* (1959)
Blohm & Voss	German	*Eagle* (1936)
Bowdler, Chaffer & Co.	British	*Sunbeam* (1874)
Brown, J., & Co.	British	S.Y. *Sapphire* (1912) S.Y. *Nahlin* (1930) R.Y. *Britannia* (1954)
Brown, W. H.	American	*America* (1851)
Cambridge, S. J. P.	British	*Lively Lady* (1948)
Campbell, W. McP.	British	*Southern Cross* (1962)
Camper & Nicholsons	British	*Czarina* (1877) S.Y. *Sagitta* (1908, hull built by Day & Summers and completed by Camper & Nicholsons) S.Y. *Miranda* (1910) S.Y. *Marynthea* (1911, hull by Thorneycroft) M.Y. *Pioneer* (1913) *Shamrock IV* (1914) M.Y. *Ara* (1917) M.Y. *Crusader II* (1929) *Mouette* (1928) M.Y. *Sister Anne* (1929) *Endeavour* (1934) *Bloodhound* (1936) M.Y. *Philante* (1937) M.T. *Malahne* (1937) *Creole*; ex-*Vira* (1927) M.Y. *Philante V* (1961) *Quiver IV* (1965) *Gipsy Moth IV* (1966)
Dunston, R.	British	*Sir Winston Churchill* (1966)
Fall River Ship Building Co.	American	S.Y. *Aloha* (1910)
Fay, J. G. & Co.	British	*Satanita* (1893)
Fife, W. & Son	British	*White Heather II* (1907) *Shamrock* (1908) *Vanity* (1923) *Cambria* (1928)
Forsyth	American	*Dauntless* (1866)
Halversen, L.	Australian	*Gretel* (1962)
Heidmann, H.	American	*Carina* (1955)

Name	Nationality	Great Yachts
Henderson, D. W. & Co.	British	*Thistle* (1887, *Meteor I*) *Britannia* (1893) *Valkyrie II* (1893) *Valkyrie III* (1895) *Meteor III* (1896)
Herreshoff Manufacturing Co.	American	*Navahoe* (1893) *Vigilant* (1893) *Westward* (1910) *Resolute* (1914) *Enterprise* (1930) *Rainbow* (1934)
Hopkee	Hong Kong	*Tzu Hang* (1939)
Ingles, A. & J.	British	S.Y. *Vanadis* (1908)
King & Sons, W.	British	*Maid of Malham* (1937) *Wanderer III* (1952)
Krupp, F. Germaniawerft	German	*Meteor IV* (1909) *Meteor V* (1914) M.Y. *Nourmahal* (1928)
Luders Marine Construction Co.	American	*Weatherly* (1958)
Marvel Inc. T.S.	American	*Corsair III* (1899)
McLean & Son, H.	British	*Myth of Malham* (1947)
Minneford Yacht Yard, Inc	American	*Dorade* (1930)
Napier Bros.	British	S.Y. *Menai* (1835) S.Y. *Glowworm* (1838) S.Y. *Fireking* (1840)
Nevins, Henry B. Inc	American	*Stormy Weather* (1934) *Vim* (1939)
Pett, Peter	British	*Katherine* (1661) *Anne* (1661) *Charles* (1662) *Henrietta* (1663)
Pett, Phineas	British	*Princess Mary* (1677) *Fubbs* (1682)
Prout & Sons, G.	British	*Rehu Moana* (1963) *Tsula Maran* (1965)
Ramage & Ferguson	British	S.Y. *Liberty* (1908)
Ratsey	British	*Cambria* (1868)
Scott & Co.	British	S.Y. *Erin* (1896) S.Y. *Margarita* (1900)
Smith, I.	American	Star Class (the first 22 from 1911)
Souter, W.	British	*Surfury* (1965)

Bibliography

Blanchard, F. S., *The Sailboat Classes of North America*. Doubleday & Co., Inc., New York, 1963.
Bradford, Ernle, *The America's Cup*. Country Life Ltd., London, 1964.
Bradford, Ernle, *Three Centuries of Sailing*. Country Life Ltd., London, 1964.
Brassey, Lady, *A Voyage in the 'Sunbeam'*. Longmans, Green & Co., London, 1886.
Brassey, Earl, *The 'Sunbeam' R.Y.S.* John Murray, London, 1918.
Burnell, R. D., *Races for the America's Cup*. Macdonald & Co. Ltd., London.
Cotter, E. F., *The International book of Catamarans & Trimarans*. Kaye & Ward Ltd., London, 1967.
Chapelle, H. I., *American Small Sailing Craft*. W. W. Norton Co., Inc., New York, 1963.
Crane, Clinton, *Clinton Crane's Yachting Memories*. D. Van Nostrand Co., Inc., Princeton, New Jersey, 1951.
Crowninshield, F. B., *The Story of George Crowninshield's Yacht*. Merrymount Press, Boston, 1913.
Dixon, D., *The King's Sailing Master*. George G. Harrap & Co. Ltd., London, 1948.
Elvström, P. & Creagh-Osborne, *Expert Dinghy Racing*. Adlard Coles Ltd., London, 1963.
Heaton, P., *Yachting, A History*. B. T. Batsford Ltd., London, 1955.
Heckstall-Smith, A., *Sacred Cowes*. Anthony Blond Ltd., London, 1965.
Herreshoff, L. F., *An Introduction to Yachting*. Sheridan House, New York, 1963.
Hoyt, C. S., *Sherman Hoyt's Memoirs*. D. Van Nostrand Co., Inc., Princeton, New Jersey, 1950.
Illingworth, Capt. J. H., *Twenty Challenges for the America's Cup*. Hollis & Carter, London, 1968.
Kelley, J. D. J., *American Yachts*. Charles Scribner's Sons, New York, 1884.
Phillips-Birt, D., *Reflections on Yachts*. Nautical Publishing Co., Lymington, 1968.
Phillips-Birt, D., *British Ocean Racing*. Adlard Coles Ltd., London, 1960.
Rayner, D. A. & Wykes, A., *The Great Yacht Race*. Peter Davies Ltd., London, 1966.
Stephens, W. P., *American Yachting*. The Macmillan Co., New York, 1904.
Stephens, W. P., Swan, W. V. & Thompson, W. M., *The Yacht 'America'*. Charles Lauriat Co., Boston, 1925.
Taylor, W. H. & Rosenfeld, S., *The Story of American Yachting*. Appleton-Century-Crofts, New York, 1958.
Taylor, W. H. & Rosenfeld, S., *The America's Cup Races*. D. Van Nostrand, Princeton, New Jersey, 1958.
Teller, W. M., *The Voyages of Joshua Slocum*. Rutgers University Press, New Brunswick, New Jersey, 1958.
Wallace, W. N., *The Macmillan Book of Boating*. The Macmillan Co., New York, 1964.
White, R. & Fisher, R., *Catamaran Racing*. Cassell & Co. Ltd., London, 1968.